9 out of 10 climbers
make the same mistakes

Navigation through the maze of advice for the self-coached climber

Dave MacLeod

Copyright © 2010 by Dave MacLeod

www.davemacleod.com - blog, training advice, coaching, shop

Published by Rare Breed Productions
Ardlarach
Letterfinlay
By Spean Bridge
Inverness-shire
PH34 4DZ
Scotland

www.rarebreedproductions.co.uk

All rights reserved. No part of this book may be reproduced in
any form without written permission by the publisher.

Edition 1.0

First published January 2010

ISBN: 978-0-9564281-0-3

Book design & layout: Claire MacLeod
Cover illustration: © Simon Oxley
Editors: Claire MacLeod, Barbara MacLeod

Printed by Lightning Source in the UK and US

To Claire

Safety and responsibility

The advice in this book is to be used at the risk and responsibility of the reader. Climbing, and training for climbing is an inherently dangerous activity. This book assumes prior knowledge and training in the fundamentals of climbing safety techniques and approaches, and safe practice in sport and training. It is intended for use in parallel with other sources of more detailed knowledge and information in each sub section discussed. This book is no substitute for taking personal responsibility for the risks and benefits of climbing and training for it, and for educating oneself thoroughly in the techniques required to achieve this.

This book is for anyone ready to challenge
and change their climbing habits.

Contents

Part 3 Fear of falling: the real problem, probably...

Part 4 The other big four: attitude, lifestyle, circumstances, tactics

Part 5 What's next coach? Planning your improvement

9 out of 10 climbers
make the same mistakes

Climbing harder is not really about finding something you don't have. It's more about getting what you already have to work for you. Everyone has potential to exceed their current level in climbing, often much more than they dream of actually managing.

Everyone has time to achieve improvement in climbing. Everyone has the resources to improve at climbing, or the power to improve the resources enough to improve their climbing.

The reason it's like this is because first: it doesn't take much to see an improvement in climbing, once you make the correct choices and adopt the attitudes of those who improve. Second: what holds climbers back from making improvements is not limited resources, but mistakes in how to use and manage their resources of climbing facilities, time for climbing and energy for climbing. The interesting bit is, almost all climbers are making the same mistakes.

In this book I'm going to try to expose as many mistakes as I can and steer you back onto the path of improvement.

Barking up the wrong tree

The cover of this book sums up the frustration of so many climbers who have been a couple of times around the block with trying to get better at climbing. They've put in the hours, year in year out. They've suffered the monotony of amassing lots of whatever currency they think is most valuable for climbing hard. For some that's muscle, or numbers of routes climbed, or competition, or saving for a year off to train properly. But the results haven't materialised! They think "I've done the time and the hard grind, where is my payback?"

When these climbers ask me for the answer as a coach, it seems harsh, unpleasant and depressing to suggest they have been barking up the wrong tree. A tiny bit more muscle won't make that difference. More hours on the same board will yield only a fraction of what it did in the beginning. In another way, it's a massive weight off the shoulders. Yes, some time may have been 'wasted' on preparation and training activities that added little value. But everyone is in this same boat. No one's preparation is perfect, even the superstar's. If you have spent a lot of time seeing climbing through one lens and a coach shows you a different one, the capital you've built up in one area (maybe it's crimp strength, or climbing front on) will still be of immense value.

If you get the chance to truly see where you have been going wrong, you are lucky. First, because not everyone does. Second, because now you can start on the real weak areas, you will see real improvement.

The image of the fed-up gorilla illustrates one of the most common lenses that climbers look through to plan their training; strength. If they've seen climbing through the lens of pure strength for some time (maybe years) they are probably strong enough for their present goals. But it's hard to get them to believe it and start looking elsewhere. They want to keep looking for strength even though it's not causing the changes in their climbing they want. In this book I am pretty direct. I hope you forgive me. I want this book to really help you climb better, and this usually means taking a sledgehammer to stubbornly engrained ideas. When I'm coaching face to face at a climbing wall, I can show you how the move can be done by drawing on factors other than strength to make the move happen. In order to provoke you enough through words alone and no demonstration to really examine what options you have for improving at climbing, I need to tell it straight.

Part 1
Creatures of habit

Stuck on the basics

For 16 years, I've watched other climbers obsessively. I've looked at how they climb, listened to what they say about climbing and watched what they do to try and improve. I've watched climbers go from struggling beginner to world class athlete and unbelievable talents stumble and give up the sport.

This observation was to try to learn from their mistakes and to climb better myself. Laterally, my involvement in climbing has been as a coach too, spreading my knowledge to others via coaching in person or online through my blogs. Coaching climbers in person over the past 5 years intensified my learning about the big hurdles that keep climbers from progressing. As well as observing them, I was able to ask them about their backgrounds, attitudes, activities - everything that has shaped the climbing they do today.

All of that learning has confirmed with growing certainty in my mind one overarching message - the central message of this book: climbers are stuck on the basics, but lost in the details.

The evolution of our understanding of performance in climbing has gone like this: First, there was hardly any information - climbers soaked up every scrap of wisdom from the great climbers of the day. The first climbing improvement books had case studies from the best at the time. They were all wildly different. Some had noticed that being light was good, and ate no fat. Others noticed being strong was good and lifted a lot of weights. All random stabs in the right direction. The best of that generation, Jerry Moffatt, figured out that systematic bouldering was a very efficient way to get strong and be able to actually climb, and so outperformed the rest until they started doing the same. With so few influences it was impossible to get a good picture of what was the thing to do, except in hindsight.

Today, the problem is completely different. Thousands of exercises, activities and regimes have been described that could potentially improve your climbing. The problem is not what to do, but what to exclude. Each person's background, circumstances and influences are different and it's getting harder and harder to make sense of the barrage of information.

So what happens? People simply get lost in a sea of details. Maybe campus boarding will work, or weights, or hanging a few seconds longer, or eating some protein powder? This sets up a cycle of trying something small for too short a period to give it a chance, getting frustrated at lack of immediate results and moving onto something else. There is little trust in whether the advice is definitely correct, so you stall before it has a chance to work.

Training methods or activities that become fashionable in sport like climbing are indeed worth questioning. In some bigger sports that have more money flowing through them, the level of scientific research and shared qualitative knowledge among coaches is a lot more robust. In less high profile sports, the accepted knowledge of the day is a mix of influences from archaic traditions, what the best athletes do, and adapted techniques from other sports. This is where climbing is at right now. Development of new ideas, methods and understanding of the nature of climbing is happening really fast and there hasn't been time to refine the useful ideas and put them in proper context. So the best strategy for self-coached climbers is to really try to grasp the structure of the climbing challenge from the basics upwards. This is the only method that will allow climbers to navigate the choices out there to optimise their improvement.

By jumping into the sea of details, tips and snippets of advice, climbers lose sight of the basics. Almost all climbers are stuck on one or two big basic errors that overwhelm attempts to improve by trying random tips. The climbers themselves will almost never see these big errors, because they got them from their habits and influences. It usually takes a good coach to identify them and put them on a reliable path of improvement. Your climbing partner will never tell you that fear of falling is the real thing holding you back, because you probably learned it from them! Nothing else is likely to trigger the realisation that this is your problem unless you get a good coach, or attack your own preconceptions directly.

You'll never see those big stopper errors from reading a standard training-for-climbing book or article either. Because they are not arranged to make you see them. They simply list every possible activity you could try.

This book comes from the opposite angle. All the way through, I'll point out the errors and wrong turns off the road of improvement that almost all climbers take. Use it as a mirror - which mistakes are you making? My guess is you'll see them, but not want to accept them. It's damn hard to change habits like avoiding falling. It feels so wrong, at first. You want to find something else to change that is more comfortable; a way around the problem, not through it. The 'something else' won't work. The only alternative to the short term pain of cracking a bad habit is keeping on staying stuck. Identifying your big basic errors and having the courage to attack them will mean that the sea of details in climbing can start to make a difference. It's your choice.

The first thing to understand

Is that any aspect of your life could be very different. Scary thought. Often the biggest difficulties in coaching climbers, especially those that want to make big changes in their ability in the long term, is for them to actually consider changes in their life, of any type. They are too scared. We are conditioned to defend against unknowns and avoid them wherever possible. When you started out climbing, everything felt free and light. There was nothing to lose. We jumped on buses with friends from School or Uni or a club and went off to new places and learned something about climbing every time. We spent time in the climbing wall, learned to climb better on a certain wall or angle after lots of practice on that same wall. Some concentrated effort paid off! A good feeling. But eventually, the improvement in that one wall/ crag/angle/type of climbing levelled off and it got boring.

So you try to find a way to break the plateau. But you can't change everything now - all of a sudden you have something to lose. If you tried something new, like bouldering, or steep overhanging routes, you would be terrible at them. It would be embarrassing! Even worse you'd lose ground on the one thing you cling onto that you can do well.

This story is the way most climbers get stuck. It's natural and human. Fear of loss, no matter how small shouts much louder than the gains on offer from taking an unknown chance on trying something new. It's also a downward spiral of morale. Most climbers hide it well, saying the accept they were never meant to climb well, or pinning the lack of improvement on something like lack of time or an injury. Others will carry on, out of habit, until a change of circumstances takes them temporarily away from climbing and maybe they just never come back.

This fear of loss is the first and largest hurdle to get past to improve at climbing. The more years you've been climbing and the more engrained your habits are, the more sensitive you'll be to changing the routine you are settled in (hint: so don't put it off!).

Most of the time, the fear of a change in the status quo can only be overcome when it is forced upon you. People have all sorts of massive life changes forced on them all the time. Illness, poverty, anything that changes the rules and your outlook on life instantly. What happens? The status quo is broken and people start adapting to the new rules, whatever they are.

In climbing, people often search out one-to-one coaching only when they reach crisis point. Fear of loss of performance or of private or public status has pushed them further and further down the cul-de-sac of controlling everything in their climbing, avoiding new things and inventing reasons not to try them. Ultimately, they realise their comfort zone has shrunk to nothing. They still want to climb, but they have finally let go of the fear to change everything, and so look for some help. With good coaching applied, every time the story is the same: climbers are shocked by how easy it is to embrace a new outlook and dive into activities that would previously have been out of the question.

For now at least, they are open to improvement. They understand that they can change how, when, what they climb and that this attitude is the foundation of new learning and improvement. Down the line, they will face the same narrowing feeling of fear of losing the gains they are making right now. Staying open to improvement and free of fear of change takes constant attention. Very few master it consistently through a whole career in sport.

The first thing to change

Is fear of change. Change opens up the possibility of failure, and fear of failure is a very basic fear. More than half of the climbers I've coached are very strong (physically) for the grades they climb and are already more than strong enough to realise their goal grades. Yet they are the ones totally focused on fine tuning their climbing/training gains to squeeze out that extra smidgen of strength. It's barking up the wrong tree. The real reason they are totally focused on strength is because deep down they are avoiding their real weakness which is usually either fear of falling, or fear of failure. But how does fear of failure show itself in climbers?

Well, it takes different forms. Here are some examples:

- Uncomfortable while climbing with others watching or even just present.
- Getting attached to 'reference' routes you know well and use to measure current fitness levels, but using them far too often.
- Putting off trying desired routes until you feel fitter, but never feeling fit enough.
- Regularly getting frustrated and angry at your climbing performances.
- Uncomfortable talking or even thinking about time-framed climbing goals.
- You think: "I'll not do this route just now because I fell off it before and they are watching me right now. I'll do that other route instead because I can cruise it."

The problem here is that most climbers who have a fear of failure problem don't actually know they have. So how do you know? To be honest it's not easy without access to an objective source of feedback who doesn't mind hurting your feelings. If your mindset is far from the ideal attitude to failure, or the above examples strike a chord in you, then you should probably see it as a problem and start attacking it.

The ideal attitude is that failure is an absolutely integral and central part of any worthwhile endeavour and of breaking performance barriers in sport. Failure can and should be relished as a psychological tool to motivate, a practical source of essential feedback for those who don't have a coach and even the spice that makes eventual success taste so sweet when it finally comes.

In my opinion there is much confusion about the place and role of failure in western society that has spilled over into sport with poor consequences for its participants. It has become an increasing norm that failure generally is bad, unacceptable and even punishable. If governments fail to meet targets, they are booted out. If football managers fail to win the league, they are sacked. Make a professional error, and your ass is getting sued etc. Watch a TV show like 'The Apprentice' and you see reams of smart folk keeping a straight face while they announce that they simply don't accept personal failure. But there is a fairly simple detail missed out here. It's fine to settle for nothing less than personal success *in the long run*. But temporary failure is the essential part of long term success. That bit gets dropped off in the edit. It wouldn't make good TV or a good headline sound-bite.

As always for any training intervention, the only way to solve this modern and common tendency is to attack it head on. This should happen first with a dramatic reorientation towards what failure means, followed by immersing yourself as pro-actively as possible in training situations featuring eventual success on top of repeated temporary failures.

The reorientation should centre around the idea that 'failure to fail' regularly in climbing is the ultimate failure to realise one's potential. The practical part is to actively seek out those situations that really expose you to your weakest, most amateur climbing limitations, publicly as well as privately. Tell people your goals. Make sure they know when you aim to have them completed. You won't manage all of them or maybe even any. And make sure you admit publicly that you couldn't manage them (this time at least). Pick the climbing situation you'd least like others to watch, and climb with as many people watching as possible. If they are filming or taking photos too, that's even better. My own fear-of-failure buster is hot, humid climbing walls. I've found that my ability drops drastically compared to many others in this situation, and I'll get brutally burned off by climbers I could out climb in almost any other situation. So I make myself have a session in a busy warm bouldering wall with locals who have the problems wired at least every couple of months.

Fail, and prepare to succeed

The psychological effect of this 'therapy' is to let go of the spectre of failure. You win back that feeling of having nothing to lose you had as a beginner. You are not perfect; you make mistakes, you pedal your feet, wobble, shout 'watch me' in a high pitched voice and fall off. It's easy to forget that everyone does. However, if this failure washes over you as it should, you can get on with the real tasks of understanding climbing better. Through failure you will be able to see your own systematic errors, receive reminders about them and eventually overcome them. Through public failure, you will open yourself to nuggets of objective advice from friends and learn something new about your own abilities. Regular failure is the essential tool for coaching yourself in sport.

If only I knew now what I knew then

Here is one message for young climbers, and one for adults.

There are some revealing comparisons to be made between the dynamics of fear of failure in adults and youngsters as they learn climbing. Focus is the main problem for young climbers, apart from the lucky few who discover its power before adulthood. In fact most young climbers reading will probably have judged it too involved and switched off already. Kids at the wall try a bit of this and a bit of that, and if it takes longer than three seconds to find the correct footholds and body position they lose patience and jump for the hold and let their light bodies swing out below them. Adults look on with jealousy at how they hold on and keep going with such obviously poor technique. But of course they pay for such reliance on temporary lightness when they grow into heavy adult bodies and have to learn good footwork with slow learning adult brains.

So the best young climber after the first few years will end up being the one who learns to focus earliest.

But what adults gain in knowing how to discipline themselves and focus on both immediate and longer term tasks, they lose in fear of failure. They become all sensitive that strangers at the climbing wall, their mates or the coach will see them wobble, flail and fall. Without knowing they are doing it, they size up potential climbs to try based on likelihood of embarrassing themselves, rather than anything else. The result? An ever narrowing comfort zone that feels progressively more unpleasant to be outside as the feedback loop plays out over time.

Kids, on the other hand, are learning everything for the first time. They are not yet masters of anything. So failing, grappling, and trying again is all they know. As soon as adults become masters in any one field (such as their job, academic field, driving, whatever) they like that feeling and settle into its comfort. Sadly, this makes it much more difficult to learn other skills at the optimum rate.

The best (and happiest) adult climber is the one who learns to focus before being an adult, and doesn't forget that failing repeatedly is normal.

Too embarrassed to climb?

So what can you do if you did forget that failure is normal and that everyone wobbles and falls (and so it's okay for you to do it too)? Being too embarrassed to climb hard in public situations is crippling for a lot of climbers' improvement and once you have it, it's hard to reverse.

You can beat it using the same techniques people use to overcome other addictions. In this case, you should see your embarrassment as being an addiction to the comfort of nobody watching. Usually, climbers can climb freely with certain people watching. It might be those at a lower level, or their climbing partners. If you can handle them seeing you struggle, you can handle everyone else too.

There are two ways to attack the problem: head on, or drip by drip. Which you choose depends on your personality. In either case the time to act is always now. The longer you've had the habit of being embarrassed by public climbing, the harder it gets to reverse. Putting it off for one more session nearly always means you'll put it off indefinitely.

Attacking it head on by jumping in at the deep end is the quickest and most effective method but doesn't always work for everyone (especially the worst cases). Most climbers will convince themselves that the apparently easier drip by drip method of exposure will work better for them. It's less often the easy option because it takes far more commitment over time and has the potential to be demoralising when you don't keep up the momentum and slip back to the starting place.

To attack it head on, it's crucial to think through how others see your climbing, and the effect of your expectations of yourself. Climbers often have unrealistic expectations of themselves, for example to be able to reproduce a previous highpoint of performance after a layoff. This unrealistic expectation turns into a worry that others will notice how badly you are climbing right now. So the first step is to be really honest with yourself about the true level of your climbing, and how restricted it is to certain strengths you have, such as a particular angle, rock type or venue. Accept personally that you won't be able to match your expectations right now, and bring them down.

The next step is to think about how you see others' climbing in order to understand how little your performance ultimately matters to them. Think of a climber you know who is climbing less than their best ever right now, or whom you know worries about their public climbing performances. How much do you care and how much time have you spent with their performance in mind? Most climbers notice the level of those around them, but don't really care what that level is. They only care about how their own performance relates. While others will notice how hard and how well (or poorly) you climb, they don't really give much thought to it. If you climb well, they'll be impressed and some may even be jealous. If you climb poorly, they just won't really notice at all.

A useful mindset to adopt is that of the underdog. The underdog is always in the psychologically less stressful position than those with a reputation to uphold in their own mind. Even if you are used to performing relatively well in your climbing (or at least think you are), you can use a wobbly performance in public to your own advantage. You can imagine that those who watched you will realise you are actually human just like them and make mistakes, even big ones. Imagine that their new expectations of your climbing are lower and so yours can follow. This will free you from worry about mistakes consuming your attention during your climbing and allow you to focus on trying hard, even if it lets your guard down to the possibility of a wobble or a fall.

If you are ready to adopt these attitudes to your own and others perception of your climbing, you might be able to make a leap in confidence by jumping in at the deep end. If you choose a climbing situation that intimidates you most and expose yourself to it fully, you might be able to cut away that self-consciousness in one go and feel you've made a fresh start.

Although this works for some, for the worst cases it might just be too much to handle, and a drip by drip gradual exposure to stressful public climbing situations is the only realistic way. It's a harder road to take because it's tough when your progress is not always linear and you have to climb back up from the bottom rung of the ladder repeatedly. But at least you only have to take small steps at a time, so making them is not so off-putting.

Those steps could be just climbing with a new partner, or on a busier night at the climbing wall, or an easy lead when you are used to toproping, or a different panel at the climbing wall you feel less confident on. Focus on one of these variables at a time and stick with it for a few sessions until you are ready to add another variable.

Above all, don't deny that a fear of public climbing or of embarrassing yourself has the power to completely halt your improvement in climbing and make it less and less enjoyable, so much so that some end up stopping climbing because of it. It's human to feel this fear but it's possible to overcome it too, and essential to do it now and not later if you want to experience improvement.

Is this grade a success or mediocre?

If you ask ten climbers who've had a career stretching several decades what was going on at the time when they were climbing their lifetime best level, odds are they'll all mention the same thing, probably before anything else: "There were loads of good people around at that time." You just can't divorce sporting performance from the fact that we are social beings and other people are often the catalysts or the downright driving forces behind our finest moments.

It's not always true for the most driven athletes who, under certain circumstances, operate better in relative isolation. However, the vast majority of climbers are likely to climb better if we are surrounded by good examples and people we like and who can help us access good climbing more often. Those with individualist driven tendencies should resist the tendency to worry about this fact of human nature. Milk it instead.

It is quite amazing how much we are influenced by the people around us and the prevailing social norms. It happens in every sphere of life. Climbing is no different. Have you ever ended up bouldering with some new people at the wall and found yourself picking up their habits? I have a friend who climbs with a very positive-aggressive technique style. My normal style is quite fast but careful. After a day out with him I find myself naturally climbing more like him. We are incredibly limited by our own inhibitions and habits and they work on us without us even noticing. When doing strength research in a sport science lab it never fails to amaze me the immediate effect on a subject's muscular output just from screaming "COME ON!" at them. And yes, the effect has been soundly proven. Basically you are saying; "It's okay to let your guard down and give it your all."

Taking the UK as an example, the national average standard for climbers is very low – VS/HVS from what I gather. Would VS climbers plateau at this grade if 90% of climbers were at E4 instead? It takes a bit of courage to break out of the normal culture – it takes either some individual thinking, or exposing yourself to the desired social norm more often.

Interacting with as many people, places, habits, and resources as possible that have a social norm that oozes a high standard of quality, performance, effort, whatever the variable, will work its way into your norms. Yes, believe it or not, if you spend all your time climbing with good climbers (good in some respect, not necessarily grade, maybe just effort level) it rubs off on you without you even knowing it. It's quite a marvellous feeling when it happens. If none of your climbing mates train, will you go and train on your own while they go to the pub? If you live in the Spanish Basque country and everyone trains (and hence climbs 8c including the females these days), will you stick at VS? Of course there is a balance to be struck between your climbing goals compromising the places and people you spend your time with, but most people's balance has room to shift a little. You only get one life and there are many paths through it; you might as well choose a good one. For most, widening the net of partners you climb with and just being aware of their negative influence will be enough to help you nurture better norms for yourself and set a nice balance between one type of fun (improving at climbing) and other types.

In general, the best influences will be other climbers who have greater knowledge, ability, keenness, an encouraging and supportive spirit and are just good fun to be with. Their good company will help motivate you on those inevitable days when doing the duller elements of climbing training seems so futile. That said, hooking up with a partner too much at the opposite end of the scale from you might not always help. If your default approach to climbing and life is chilled out and spontaneous then teaming up with the most driven and relentless personalities might become hard work in the long term.

Friendly competition is a very important catalyst and a highly enjoyable aspect of climbing in its own right. So climbing with good people will both make your climbing a richer and happier experience as well as help you get better at it faster.

This is quite self-evident I suppose. My main message here is not to underestimate it's effect. If you are feeling that motivating yourself to work harder at your climbing is not coming easily, don't make other people your last port of call to find the answer. Make it the first call you make.

The first generation was the freest

Let's take another look at rock climbing history. The first generation of climbers to really go for it with training - Wolfgang Gullich, Jerry Moffatt, Ben Moon, Malcolm Smith and their contemporaries set the bar so high it's taken another full generation just to consolidate that level. Routes like Action Direct 9a and Hubble 8c+ (old school 8c+, that is) are still seeing off the very best in sport climbing 20 years later. Why is that?

It's because of the conditions at the time those climbers were operating in. There were no norms to conform to, nothing to settle for. They knew they wanted to get good and advance standards, and because they were the first to enjoy the breakthroughs of training in climbing, they knew they could take standards forward. But by how much? They were not training regularly with a large group of peers, so they had nothing to measure their level of effort against but their own perception of effort and commitment.

When you are relatively isolated from information to help measure your progress, it's harder to settle for less effort. You can only imagine your peers out there are working harder than you are and that feeling drives you on.

Climbers today can never have the same conditions. Everyone can get to a climbing wall, build a board, hang off an edge and find access to information on how to train. It's everywhere. So if your peers stop training and head for the pub, it's easy to imagine everyone does. If you just out-climbed your regular partner, it's hard not to sit back and wallow. So what to do?

Two choices: One choice would be to make a clear decision to separate yourself from the norms of the climbers you know and that your level of effort is going to be much higher. That way, you'll have the best chance not to give in to settling for less and you'll look to your own internal measures of how hard you are trying. The other choice is to seek out the company of those who you know are trying the hardest. It could be someone at your climbing wall, a coach, or a video of a famous climber. Keep reminding yourself of their level of effort, either by climbing with them all the time, watching their video again or just watching them climb at the wall. Use them as your benchmark.

Young talented climbers suffer the most from this problem. They quickly become the best in their peer group and their local wall. So they think they are really trying hard. Usually it's when they take their first trip to a famous sport crag or an international competition that they have a massive shock - they thought they knew how to give it everything, but they are nowhere. It's enough to make some give up the sport. If they looked around earlier for better role models, they could be up there already.

Starting from scratch

So you've decided to start from scratch, to go for it with a fresh effort to break out of a plateau. The feeling is hard to sustain isn't it? In many older climbers (those who have been climbing for over a decade – so could still be teenagers!) I've coached, I've detected a rather jaded attitude to 'starting afresh' with an all new plan of action to lick their form into shape. The trouble with starting from scratch is they've been here before, most probably every November when they hit the climbing wall again, or every April when they realise they are still struggling on the same grade they were last year and the five before that.

Starting from scratch on a merry-go-round period of hard work, with some results, followed by an imperceptible doldrums where you gradually slip back to the starting place is soul destroying, don't you think?

I'm not about to tell you there is a magic way round the interruption to your sport and training caused by the 'one off' extra hours at work, DIY jobs, and the million other things that take their place, rightly or wrongly, at the top of the priority list. But the loss of previous hard earned gains in fitness is avoidable. Simply by exploiting a simple feature of how our bodies respond to training stimulus, we can have our cake and eat it.

The feature I'm talking about is cryptically referred to as 'reversibility maintenance'. It turns out much less stimulus is needed to maintain a given level of fitness than to increase it. The amount of training we are talking about obviously depends a bit on your level, but for many of you it will be in the region of one session per week. The main thing is to re-orientate your idea of training to include this idea: not all training activity is about immediate improvement. For parts of the year, you are just training to tread water for later. It's longer term thinking. It's a day in, day out part of training for athletes. But in amateur sport it's massively under-used and under-prescribed.

When most climbers have a super busy period, for instance, an autumn where you change jobs, move house and four weekends get filled up with mate's weddings, they just give in, and stop climbing altogether until the dust has settled. The rationale is usually, "I'll just get frustrated if I try to fit climbing in with all this going on, so I'll just forget about it for the time being." I understand the psychology, but it only helps in the short term. Sure, stopping altogether will make it easier to pass the time until you have your leisure back, but when you start again six months down the line and feel weak and unfit, this always delivers a secondary and more severe motivational blow - "What's the point of starting to climb this fitness ladder from the bottom, all over again?"

The feeling has been strong enough in a few climbers to make them leave the sport altogether. Yet it's unnecessary. It's great to be open with yourself and accept when three sessions a week of climbing are going to be off the cards for a while. Instead of stopping dead, this time figure out what time you could manage per week. It doesn't matter how small the amount of time is, so long as it's as much as you can spare and it's realistic.

For those few minutes or hours per week, you'll switch mindset from your normal outlook on climbing/training of, "I am trying to improve" to, "I am trying to maintain my current level." Just this simple change of attitude will make it much easier to discipline yourself to stick to it for the weeks and months of being busy.

The result of this is that when things calm down again, you can pick up where you left off and start working to the next grade with refreshed motivation and a rested body, instead of trying to force an unfit body to build back up too quickly (which often causes injury, never-mind frustration).

Of course, there is more to it than just deciding you are going to do some maintenance training for a while. The practicalities form the next immediate hurdle. For some, a brief escape to a local climbing wall once a week is possible. Great! If not, you'll have to train at home. This option is a lot better than it sounds for the time poor - there is no travelling time involved.

Training at home requires a home climbing board (for those with space and inclination) or a simple wooden strip fingerboard on a door-frame. Climbers these days seem fairly resistant to the idea of having a facility at home, usually due to cost, permission problems, or getting bored trying to use them. All of these issues are fairly simple to side-step. The beauty of working on a small home board or fingerboard is that it's well suited to short sessions snatched while the tatties boil or while watching the evening news. Little and often is what reminds your fingers to stay strong because next season you will be back to normal. More on this later in the book.

Everyone has busy periods, but they don't have to force you back to beginner level. Tread water with one session per week instead and pick up where you left off instead of going to square one.

The truth about famous climbers

They aren't really much better than you are, yet their grades, results, level, rewards somehow end up being absolutely miles higher than you have managed.

Watch some world class climbers in a climbing DVD making the performance of their life, on a climb they've spent years preparing for and trying. It looks perfect. It's as close as it gets. It creates an incorrect image of these climbers though. Understand that you are seeing the pinnacle - a concentrated shot of so many ingredients brought together into the final ascent (with the excuse filled bad days, foot slips and whinges about bad conditions edited out).

If you want some real inspiration, you need to observe some good climbers over time. Some might indeed be super strong, but they can't use their feet well. Others may be technical masters, but get them on a brutal power move and you'll be shocked how weak they are. It's not inspiring because the famous climbers are real heroes, it's because they aren't! They really are just like you and me, but they still pull off the apparently impossible.

What is going on here?

It comes down to this:

4% less effort does not get you 4% less results.

Often, 4% less effort gets 90% less results.

The return on making that little extra effort is vastly out of proportion with the extra work required. Multiply this across all the disparate aspects of climbing performance, and 4% extra in each one delivers a windfall of results that lifts you over huge barriers of performance.

In practice?

A top climber will try the boulder problem 26 times for your 25, and do it on the last go.

A top climber will rest 20 seconds less per attempt on the climbing wall problem than you. (Hint: multiply the extra attempts by the number of sessions per year, or per decade to see the significant effects of this on total training load).

A top climber will hang on five seconds longer than you before shouting 'take' and see the move to get them through to that next shakeout, and then the top.

There are a million examples of how this plays out in practice. Each single one seems trivial, but taken together the effect explains why the best manage what they do, and you don't.

So, is it as simple as all that? Just try a bit harder, hang on a bit longer, do that extra route, go for that hold a bit more aggressively, and that'll do the trick? Yes, but it's not something to try for a few months, like a diet, or a phase of endurance circuits. The rewards are massive but come chunk by chunk, building up from tiny steps over years before you are that climber who has just enough of every ingredient to produce a brilliant performance.

Know your enemy - your tastes

It's a natural human trait to seek out comfort. It's a natural human trait to centre our activities around skills we are particularly good at. But success in sport is knowing how to use our best assets at the right moment, but not revelling in them to the point we leave ourselves with weaknesses.

'Work your weaknesses' is commonly said in training advice, but it's easier said than done. This is especially true over the long term, when regular habits and routines of all types become established in your climbing activity. The best climber is likely to be the one whose routines and habits are constantly broken up by either travel or the influence of constantly changing partners. These lucky climbers learn to take comfort in the fact that the climbing diet they feed themselves will constantly change. They don't get the opportunity to get settled into well defined preferences and tastes in any aspect of their climbing (e.g. the angle, rock type, hold type, ascent style, schedule, among countless other variables).

Your climbing will naturally tend to fall into a routine either due to the climbing venues, or partners and schedules that are limited by your circumstances. When this happens, it's really hard not to fall into working your strengths without consciously fighting it.

It takes conscious effort to recognise the types of climbs, moves, angles, any aspect of the climbing experience that you find yourself drawn to for what they really are - a vulnerability to opening up weak points in your climbing. Of course you should enjoy and regularly do the types of climbing you are good at. Instead of subconsciously falling into doing them all the time, see them more as a delight to be savoured but not overindulged.

Play a mental game where you see performance areas you know you are weak on as a treat because any exposure to them will quickly yield more substantial gains than any other aspect of your game. This way, you'll find it easier to overcome the gravitational pull of preferences, tastes and routines.

My guess is that you've heard the idea of working weaknesses many times before, think you have internalised it and even put some effort in to doing it. But very few climbers apply it consistently over any length of time. Instead, they get stuck in comfortable habits. The idea of working your weaknesses is both fairly simple and strong for those trying to improve at any multifaceted skill like climbing. So why then is it so ineffective in galvanising people to do just that?

Partly, it's the sheer strength of our tendency towards comfort, fear of the unknown and fear of potential loss of what you currently have by trying something new. But I also sense that the full consequences of getting stuck in habits and not attacking weaknesses are not fully understood. People tend to think of 'weaknesses' as static entities in the background. Their influence, although negative on performance, is neither increasing or disappearing while we ignore them. We keep ignoring them because of the apparent pain in attacking them and because we feel we can still achieve improvement by working within the comfort zone (strengths that we enjoy working on). In other words we feel "at least my weaknesses are not getting any worse" while we ignore them.

Unfortunately, performance strengths and weaknesses are not static, independent forces. Spending time working in the comfort of your strengths or relying on them (maybe it's crimping, or bold runouts, or delicate slabs) borrows strength from your best assets or talents. But borrowing strength builds weakness. Weaknesses grow faster as you ignore them than you can grow your strengths by attempting to reinforce them.

Sticking with what's comfortable isn't a slow steady way to improve. It's a slippery slope that starts off too shallow to notice, but steepens alarmingly down the line.

Don't get stuck

Improvement in climbing has no shortcuts. Work has to be done, and knowledge of body movements, tactics and choosing the correct activities has to be digested piece by piece over time.

The nature of the path from beginner to mastery in any one component skill doesn't make it any easier. In your first steps in learning a new skill, any strategy brings immediate improvement, every session. Trial and error, copying others or reading the basics brings satisfying progress. Until the dip happens. The term was coined by Seth Godin and neatly describes the huge gulf between the end of that initial rush of improvement and hard won mastery. When it appears to take 10,000 hours of practice to go from beginner level to world class mastery in complex skills like sport or playing musical instruments, even tiny improvements seem to take forever to occur once you get past the initial rush of learning the basics. And when the improvements do happen, they are inconsistent and there might be long periods when that particular component skill falls short of a previous highpoint.

While lost in the middle of the dip, it's natural to doubt you are on the right path, to question your methods and consider quitting and switching to another tack. The delight of beginner's progress seems a distant memory, the powerful sense of mastery seems not even on the horizon and all you feel are the (immediate) symptoms of the battle weary.

The need to question the wisdom of all this effort is useful. Sometimes, quitting and doing something else really is the thing to do. If it's the wrong dip, no amount of effort and time will break through to the huge yield of mastery.

Trying to learn excellent mental focus, toughness and boldness for climbing from partners who are constantly negative, unreliable and unmotivated might be an endless dip. Trying to climb statically to get around a fear of falling is an endless dip. The end of your tether, and failure is the guaranteed destination of these examples, eventually. So the sooner you quit and switch to a better path, the better. For most, the idea of changing, or giving up on a habit they believe in is too painful, so they continue, stuck.

The problem is that sometimes being in the right dip can feel like being stuck too, like hanging onto the idea of climbing a certain grade. Year after year, and you still haven't made it. Maybe you just can't do it with all the limitations you have - job, family, location, facilities? It's easy to be consumed by the symptoms of weariness from sustained hard effort, drowning out the signals of progress that come imperceptibly slowly.

Some climbers fail to reach big goals because they are stuck in a dip they ought to quit, like campus boarding their way to the highest grades, or climbing statically, or trying to learn good footwork with bad rockshoes. But sometimes, they falter in the middle of a dip that will yield the results they are looking for. They fold under the strain of fatigue, impatience or short term thinking. Perhaps the biggest dip is a willingness to keep looking for areas you are worst at, and attacking them head on without delay or hesitation, day in day out. That takes real commitment and vision to see the climber you are turning into, piece by piece, struggle by struggle over years. The rest of the book will help you see many more dips to quit, and more to stick with.

Creatures of habit

Any climbing technique, tactic, or routine we use is just a habit. Our climbing ability is a composite of all of these many habits put together. The best climber is the one who has adopted the most habits that result in good performance. Each time we act out each of these habits, from the way we place our foot on a hold to what thoughts we have during a climb, we reinforce them. Their influence becomes more consistent and more difficult to break (but never impossible to break, thankfully). Engrained bad habits make climbers' experience work against them at least as much as it does for them. Most climbers can see their biggest bad habits by themselves, but feel powerless to change them: "I just can't do overhangs!"

The strength to escape the gravitational pull of habits and the sense of inevitability they impose on you is hard. However, understanding that the alternative, that the dull ache of plateau is harder still, will help to sharpen your appetite to change. But it's not just the will to actually break habits that's hard (actually that's only hard to start, but like a dam breaking, once you break the wall, everything else follows easily, for a while at least). Many climbers are at a loss of how to begin changing bad habits. Breaking habits requires three ingredients for change:

- The desire to change.
- The knowledge of what to change.
- The skills to make the change.

Some good habits, like some advanced aspects of movement technique, require new knowledge and skills that benefit from support, like reading this book, watching other good climbers, or getting some coaching in climbing movement. Others can be learned intuitively by just 'doing'. Simply adopting the habits of those who are good at that aspect will yield most of the necessary improvement, in time. Those who say "I just can't do overhangs!" have convinced themselves they have no way forward and so rarely try, at least for long enough to see any improvement. Those who are good at overhangs climb a lot of overhangs. Simple, but people don't readily connect the two phenomena. Climb a lot of overhangs, for long enough, and you cannot fail to improve at them. However, most people get stuck in the dip and go looking for something else instead, usually back in their comfort zone.

Finding more bad habits to substitute in this way is the next difficult hurdle. Doing climbing is hard enough: analysing it and identifying the correct choices in a sea of options and areas of expertise is another level. This book will identify many of the most important and common habits that climbers would benefit from changing.

Actually changing engrained habits is desperately hard for most people. And the longer you've had the habit or the older you are, the harder it will be - so start now! However, the 'stuck in your ways' disadvantage of the old is sometimes balanced out by a stronger will, sharpened by a sense of urgency of time marching on and the dull ache of a long performance plateau. Take advantage of this feeling.

Part 2
The big four:

movement technique
finger strength
endurance
body mass

The biggest lesson from sport science

Is perspective. Those who end up getting the most improvement keep an eye on the bigger picture of what influences their level, and keep perspective about how much time and energy to devote to each component.

Most climbers don't appreciate the effect of the whole range of performance variables in climbing. In fact they only see a fraction of them. And what's worse is they have a skewed idea of their relative importance, based on their own limited experiences, influences and tastes.

The big four components of ability to climb rock are movement technique, finger strength, finger endurance and body mass. Among the many other components, these are the most important. Out of the four, it's in fashion right now to overrate the importance of finger strength compared to the others. Of course it's important - your fingers can never be strong enough in climbing. The other aspects are not generally valued enough.

However, that's only part of the picture.

Climbing success is about climbing routes successfully. And the skills for climbing routes add up to more than just ability to make moves on rock. Completing routes needs further attributes that are commonly neglected by climbers - tactics and mental skills (especially fear of falling). It's one thing discussing how to train 'the big four', but the training volume is often severely stunted by failure to set up the correct circumstances. I'm talking about arranging the correct facilities, a good routine that makes the most of your time, a good lifestyle so you are not too stressed, under slept, undernourished or hungover to actual handle any training to speak of. You'll also need to have your life well arranged to deal with inevitable setbacks like injury, time-swallowing life events, problems with motivation and reaching a simple balance between sport and everything else in life to stay happy, motivated and focused.

Young, fit, eager climbers don't want to hear about all that stuff though! They only want to know the best workout on the fingerboard. Little do they know that all 'that stuff' is what is going to stop them reaching their dream routes, down the line.

The best climber is the one who puts all four of the big four climbing performance variables (not just finger strength now boys) at the heart of their climbing preparation, but also spends time thinking and applying effort to all the other aspects, today. Not when it's too late. The 'big four' are 'big', but they are not everything.

You cannot break the laws

The world of sport science observed how humans worked, learned, succeeded and failed in mastering sports. It discovered through careful observation, then systematic research how the body and mind respond in a characteristic way and so developed an understanding of several core principles of how to maximise improvement in sport. A foundation that informs all decisions about choosing the best activities to focus on at any given time. Together with listening to the messages from your body, and having knowledge of the range of techniques to be learned, they are all you need to plan the optimum improvement. Despite the fact that they are common knowledge and often referred to among coaches with a background in sport science, their massive importance remains almost invisible in the general discourse among climbers about improvement in their sport.

It doesn't help that their common names sound a bit non-descript to those not already familiar with the concepts. A succinct explanation brings their meaning to life a little:

Specificity - What you do, you become. Your performance is the product of your everyday habits.

Overload - To improve, you must do more than before to stimulate the body. However, the 'more' can be achieved by adjusting several different variables.

Reversibility - Use it or lose it. But only a little work can maintain fitness or skill in a given variable.

Variety - The body needs fresh and new stimulus to keep responding. The variety needed might be more subtle than you realise.

Individuality - What works for the next person probably won't for you.

Everyone ends up with different weaknesses and so different priorities.

As with any basic, unalterable principle of our makeup or environment, we cannot break these laws. We can only break ourselves against them. And that's exactly what tends to happen.

The reason for this is that other aspects of our character, personality or outside influences constantly leads us off the path set by these guiding principles. I'm talking about impatience, fear, self-consciousness, ego, procrastination, ignorance, or engrained habits. The effect of the social influences within the sport is not to be underestimated. Even those who tend to show great strength of character and a strong willingness to educate themselves thoroughly in the principles of learning the skills are subject to great pressure to conform to the norms of the sport's social atmosphere.

You can see this in action by looking around at other sports, or better still participating in them. In certain sports it's considered normal among participants to cheat when you can get away with it (EPO abuse in cycling), or to value strong ego as a positive performance trait (boxing), or to subscribe to very simplistic and heavy handed training methods. Standing back as an outsider, it's easy to see how these social fashions within the closed group of a sport hold it back. So it's no surprise when successful sports people often cite previous life experience in a different sport or arena of human endeavour as the 'secret' to them overtaking the level of the entrenched performers they have beaten.

Let's take the most socially charged word I used above as an example - ignorance. Visit one country or climbing wall or area and you'll find climbers who feel that doing 10 pitches of climbing in a day is a lot. How did they arrive at this figure? It didn't happen by rigorous experimentation, trying to climb more, and manipulating the quality of other variables like recovery and recording the effects on the body over time. It's just what they know. It's been passed to them as an acceptable number of climbs to count as 'a lot'. So when they travel and see other groups of climbers who climb ten pitches as the warm-up, then do their hard redpoints, then go running, they are awestruck! It's a reality check.

Do such striking differences occur? Yes they do, but it's not down to one variable being different. The culture in one group of sportspeople is made up of many skills and knowledge they share with each other. Techniques, tactics, planning and recovery strategies commonly used all play their part in way the actual sporting activity and the results achieved are shaped.

Thankfully, sharing in skills and knowledge hard won by groups of climbers around the world is easier than it's ever been. So the challenge for today's climber is to follow the principles of training, screen out the negative influences that threaten to pull you off the path of improvement, while tuning into as many positive influences as possible, and ultimately, the messages from your body.

How to learn technique

Most climbers these days understand that their climbing would improve and they would get more out of their present level of strength and fitness if they learned to move better and more efficiently on the rock. In the past few years the sport has really started to accept that to achieve this, climbers need to pay attention to good examples and influences from which to copy good movement technique. Good examples might be climbing coaches, or just good climbers you can watch in the flesh or on videos.

So now, the stumbling block is knowing what practical things climbers can do to teach themselves good technique. Climbers tell themselves, "I'm going to climb this hard route and consciously focus on my technique." But it doesn't work! And what's more it gets extremely frustrating. The conscious thought slows everything down, making you get pumped quickly. The conscious mind working with trial and error makes stupid mistakes and you fall off in a fluster. Even though you were concentrating harder than ever, it felt worse than normal, not better!

The problem is that good technique, by necessity, is automatic and most of our technical decisions while climbing have to happen outside of conscious thought. There are just too many decisions to be made from second to second to control complex body movements and accelerations in different directions. As soon as we interfere with slow, clunky conscious processing, coordination falls apart on hard climbs. The conscious mind only has room to deal with a handful of movement decisions at any one moment.

So what to do? The best time to consciously work on your basic movement technique is generally away from your limit and on easier climbs where you have more thinking space to gather and process the feedback from your body on how you are moving. Warming up is a good time, easier routes and bouldering is also good. Repetitive training on climbs you know well can also be good for fine tuning movements, although it can have negative effects of it's own if overused, as your body gets too accustomed to knowing what's coming next.

However, hard routes are important too because this is where all the pieces of the performance jigsaw must fit and work together. How do we get round the problem that we are too busy just trying to stay on the rock to worry about moment-by-moment analysis? The answer is we must do it afterwards.

Record, replay, review

A crucial skill as you advance in climbing is to be able to record what you just did and how you did it in fine detail for recall later. This is a learned skill and will take years to get really good at. But with some effort, you'll learn to work back through routes you've just done in your minds eye, and 'feel' the body feedback in retrospect. What's even better is that once you get good at this, it happens so much in the background of your mind that you don't even know you are doing it.

Replay and review of the moves you just did is also crucial to increase the volume of move information your mind deals with over time (and hence how much learning can occur). Climbing rock is a fairly short lived activity, especially sport climbing and bouldering. In a three hour bouldering session you might spend less that 30 minutes actually on the wall making moves, and the remaining time resting.

Those who spend that resting time with the mind wandering elsewhere or just getting bored waiting for their body to be ready to climb again, or for their partner to get to the top of the route, learn to climb slowly and often stop learning altogether.

Those who replay the movements of the climb just done, recording which moves felt good or bad and looking back at the holds trying to understand why, and then plan their next attempt to try the movement a subtly different way, progress fast. Both the actual climbing, and the replay and tactical planning that occurs between climbs are crucial components of the learning. These climbers are storing up move processing time at a much higher rate than the 'passive' climbers and after a couple of short years will end up with a vastly wider and more consistent move repertoire.

Next time you are in a bouldering wall and see two good climbers working on the same boulder problem, listen to what they are saying to each other between attempts. They are constantly discussing the details of each move, voicing things they experienced on their last attempt and making observations about the other's body positions and movements on their attempts. Watch how they unlock the climb's secrets through systematic experimentation and discussion of the merits and peculiarities of each subtly different way of climbing the moves. This is technique training.

No one does drills, right?

In other sports, athletes do drills. But climbers don't. Why not, and is it a problem? Yes, and here's why:

Other sports often have a distinct separation between practice and competition. Like tennis for example. Tennis players spend a lot of time hitting balls to each other as well as the actual matches. They get plenty of practice at both. What's crucial here is the mindset of 'practice'. During practice hitting, they are not trying to score points. It doesn't matter if they make mistakes. In fact making the mistakes and learning to refine the techniques from them is the whole point.

Practice is also more systematic by nature - they spend an hour practicing serves, one after another, then smashes, then lobs etc. This focus on one part of the technical repertoire at a time, together with the freedom from having to worry about competing, means real progress is made.

Climbers don't do this. The activity is not set up for it. We don't 'practice' and then 'perform'. We just 'climb'. Even when we see the climbing session as training, we still get hung up on trying to perform all the time. The result of this is basically that learning is a lot slower than it could be. We're spending all the time trying to be 100% on every aspect, and fail to learn any single one effectively. It gets even worse when we get training so confused with performing that we take extra rest days to be strong for our training sessions, lest we perform badly on a route we feel we 'should' be able to do every session. Less and less practice movements get done this way, with less attention given to the movement because we are too busy worrying about the result of the movement.

When the idea of spending some time doing technique drills is suggested to climbers, it is met with confusion or indifference. I understand why. They think - "What exactly would that entail? When would you actually do it? I've never heard of other climbers doing it..."

Both understanding what a climbing technique drill would look like, and actually incorporating it into your climbing activity are big hurdles for the imagination that most climbers just feel lost in, and so ignore. The problem is that climbing moves are comparatively undefined compared to something like a golf swing, which has a consistent ideal movement to perfect, or tennis which has a cadre of shots to give structure to practice. Climbing moves are much more varied than this, but not so much that we can't define certain key moves such as twisting to extend the shoulder and reach, rockovers, drop-knees etc.

So how can we build systematic technique drills into our climbing, without it becoming overly scientific or regimented? The first and most obvious way discussed above is during your warm-up. The climbing is below your limit, so you have mental energy left over to concentrate on the quality of the movement. Pick one thing at a time to focus on - keeping arms straighter during foot movements, foot precision, or speed or fluidity. At first you'll need to consciously tell yourself to do this to break habits of just climbing passively without thinking too much. Through sustained application, good climbers have developed the habit of concentrating (drilling) on one specific aspect in their mind and movements so much that they don't even realise they are doing it.

The second situation where technique drills commonly happen for good climbers is while working boulder problems, or sections of routes. Repeatedly trying short sections, single moves or even parts of single moves (one foot move for example) to perfect and subsequently link the moves. The mistake of some climbers is to simply try over and over, focusing their mind's energy on simply pulling harder and grabbing the next hold as quickly and accurately as possible. Delivering 100% focus on physical effort during the move is the final piece of the redpoint process, not the first. The habit of good climbers is to focus the mind simply on getting feedback from the body while trying a move, looking for parts of the body or movement that feel 'wrong'. They think of every possible way of doing the move and work through them one after the other, listening to the body feedback each time. By doing this, patterns emerge in what feels 'wrong' and what feels 'right' for that movement, that layout of holds. The result is twofold. First: the very best way to do the move is learned by elimination of poorer options. Secondly, and more importantly, the mind has been exposed to a large number of separate pieces of information about what works well and what doesn't for a particular layout of holds. All this information and learning on just one move! This way the countless attempts on moves or sequences that goes on during a session (and then a whole year of bouldering sessions) adds up to a massive number of separate technique drills, and a lot of movement learning.

So, it's about what your mind is focusing on during your climbing, forgetting about performing all the time and making more of your opportunities to turn normal climbing into technique drills.

It's possible for two identical climbers to do exactly the same session (a warm up and session of working through boulder problems or routes) but only one to experience technique drills that will make progress in technique learning. Climber 'A' thinks about what he's going to have for dinner during warm-up and thinks about nothing but pulling harder next attempt during the boulder problems. Climber 'B' chooses a specific aspect of his movement to focus on during his warm up climbs (tonight it's swapping feet). Then he consciously replays each attempt on the hard problems in his mind, looking for parts of moves that feel wrong and why (e.g. left foot seems too low). Only when he's close to the problem does he stop thinking and just give 100% physical effort to finish the problem off. And if this isn't enough, it's back to 'feedback' mode to further refine the move that's causing the fall. After three years of this, climber 'B' is a much better climber than 'A' even though they have done the same number of climbing hours.

The message: Spend more time learning climbing. Perform only at the right moment.

The structure of climbing technique

As climbers tried to better understand the nature of good movement technique in climbing over the decades, it's natural that we have assigned words that anchor our notions of what good climbing technique looks like. Two of the most important of these are 'balance' and 'control'.

They are used all the time in discourse between climbers about moves on climbs, and are certainly two foundational elements of efficient movement on rock. Although the application of simple anchoring words like these help us to stay focused on the priorities for moving well, they also have their limitations for taking understanding of movement on rock to a higher level.

'Control' brings up connotations of slow, deliberate movements, reaching carefully between hand and footholds. 'Balance', for many, brings up a similar sense of reaching a static point of balance in the body, keeping it still to be ready to move a limb to the next hold. The problem with these anchoring, descriptive words is that climbers can interpret them differently, leading to a skewed idea of the important aspects of climbing. Some climbers today still feel that moving as statically as possible between holds is an ideal way to climb.

Both words are useful at a basic, beginner level of understanding what keeps you on the rock. But as climbers move beyond the basic tasks of moving from hold to hold and need to deal with smaller, spaced and awkwardly positioned holds, they are not enough. As climbing gets harder, speed and control of movements start to become a trade-off of benefits. Both lead to efficiency in making the most of our available strength to keep going, but applying too much of one works against the other.

Speed doesn't just help by reducing the total amount of time taken to climb the route (saving energy by not having to hang on as long): it is also essential to help us move between holds that cannot be reached 'in balance', or in static balance to be more precise. When talking about balance, the idea of it is often limited to holding static positions. In the case of climbing this means finding a body position that allows you to remove a limb and replace it on the next hold slowly, without the body swinging out of control. Some moves, especially smaller ones where the hand and footholds are evenly spread out, are achieved by obtaining static balance.

However, when the holds are unhelpfully positioned or just far apart, our centre of gravity needs to move outside of the base of support (the area between our points of contact on the wall surface) to reach the next hold. When this happens, dynamic motion is needed to make the move. There is still balance, but an entirely different kind; dynamic balance. Dynamic balance uses acceleration to move our body through the correct path, outside our base of support, only coming to rest when we grab the next hold.

We initiate the move by accelerating our body, or part of it in the direction of the next hold, and make the move in balance, but at speed. Moving our body slowly (or 'statically' as climbers would call it) on big moves, where the body travels outside the base of support takes enormous force from the muscles. Use of momentum replaces the need for such huge muscle work.

The need for momentum

Those who like to climb very statically might accept that dynamic motion and momentum is required on really big moves, but what about small moves? The layout of the holds is not the only variable that affects the move. The size and usefulness of the hold does too. When the holds get poor, and just hanging on with two hands is hard enough, taking one hand off to reach slowly for the next hold becomes impossible. If we grab it quickly instead, we might be able to hold onto it before our body starts to accelerate downwards too fast.

What if we accelerated upwards and were moving at speed before we take the hand off to reach? This would reduce the need for extra force to maintain contact with one less limb during the move. By generating upward momentum before the move happens, we essentially borrow a split second from gravity to grab the next hold before our weight pulls us down again. The reduction in force requirement from the hands is not the only benefit afforded by momentum use. In fact, the greater benefit is the opportunity to generate more of the force from the lower body. It's obvious that our bodies are designed for applying the large forces of moving our bodies around using the lower limbs - the muscle groups are much larger - and the upper body, with its much smaller musculature, struggles to cope with the demands of rock climbing which require ever greater forces from the fingers as climbs get harder. The more we can keep applying energy for the moves from the lower body, even on steep ground, the better. Use of momentum in climbing allows us to drop down low while preparing to move, well inside the base of support in order to get space to accelerate. In this crouched position, bent legs are well positioned to apply force and start the move.

We feel the need to apply momentum most strongly on the really small holds. There is no other option to initiate the next move. However this momentum, and the dynamic movement that accompanies it, should also be applied even on the bigger holds, where we could do the move statically. The reason is that momentum produces efficiency. Less force is needed at the fingers and more of it comes from the lower body or momentum of the body mass that started from a lower, more advantageous position for generating force. Thus more upper body strength is saved for higher up the route. For this reason, momentum should be used on nearly every move.

The only exceptions in climbing are where you are moving from a good hold to a hold that is so small and precise that moving off it is only possible if the fingers are placed in exactly the right way, so you must take it slowly to dig the fingers into the exact right spot. The other obvious exception is where you are reaching to something you don't know is really a hold you can use, in a position where falling has serious consequences. However, even on poorly protected trad climbs, reading the rock from below will allow you to move with momentum on most moves, or just a bit more cautiously than you might on a sport climb.

Types of momentum

Despite the fact that application of momentum is the most efficient way to make climbing moves in nearly all situations, it is still very poorly understood among climbers. Ask a random selection of climbers what it means and they will give different answers, often thinking the idea refers to a high speed continuous upward movement without stopping, as you might see in a speed climbing competition.

The reality is that the momentum has to be applied in different directions; towards the rock, sideways swings and with different parts of the body, rather than a continuous upward motion. And although carrying momentum from one move into the next is an ideal, it's rarely achievable for most climbers, who cannot climb quickly enough without sacrificing too much accuracy.

So is there a convenient way to understand momentum? Although there are countless subtleties in how momentum can be applied in climbing moves, there are some basic, common body movements that help to give structure to your understanding of the principles. These make a foundation for more complex momentum use as you gain experience. As soon as you learn these basic technique drills and become aware of them, they can have a dramatic effect on the standard of your climbing if you have previously learned a static movement habit. Practice them one by one on good holds on a steep wall:

Leg thrust

The most basic momentum move in climbing. Prepare the move by hanging low from the handholds, but placing the feet high so the legs are crouched with knees fully bent. Initiate the move by dropping down fully onto straight arms and relaxed shoulders to give maximum space for the upward acceleration. Push hard with both legs to move upwards at speed and catch a hold as far as you can reach. To fully understand the effect, practice on big holds with the movement being far enough that when the move is completed, the trailing hand/hold is level with your thigh. After repeating several times dynamically, now try and do it static, and feel how much more force is needed from the hand and arm you are reaching off.

Hip swing

From the same starting position, choose a hold to aim for that is distant but well out to one side. Start the move by swinging your hips from side to side like a pendulum. Follow this swinging motion through with an even bigger dynamic swing out to the next hold. Beginners take some time to find the correct plane for the swing and to realise how pushing/pulling with alternate left and right hands/feet is used to get the swing going.

Hip thrust

On steep ground, a leg thrust is often used when the body is turned to the side in a laybacking position. But it feels more awkward when the legs and arms are more spread apart and the body is facing the rock. In this case, from the low hanging position of arms straight or nearly straight and bent legs, let the hips come away from the rock, effectively hanging your bum out in space. Then, thrust the hips inwards, towards the rock. This motion provides inward momentum at the same time as extending the body to reach the hold. Often it's applied with a slight twist of the trunk on the same side you are reaching, to aid extension of the reaching arm.

Head butt

This type of momentum is commonly used on angles around vertical where the holds are really tiny and so the body has to be kept as close to the wall as possible to stay on. Because sticking your bum out in space and swinging like the above methods would make it impossible to hold on, the only body part you can feasibly use to generate the momentum are the head and shoulders. With the hips tight-in against the wall, arch your back, letting your head and shoulders lean out from the wall (not too much). Use a gentle head butt (not too much obviously!) to throw the head and shoulders back inwards towards the wall. This inward momentum should allow a brief moment to grab the next hold. At a more advanced level, you'll find that if the hold you are going for is also very poor, you might catch it in control but not be able to hold on. Just after you catch the hold, you can buy yourself time to generate enough force on the hold by letting your head and shoulders come out again, this time decelerating.

The flick (or roll)

The roll is often used when doing a cross through move with the hands. Its purpose is to roll the trunk on its axis to extend the reaching shoulder towards the next hold. It's harder for the legs to produce this rotational force, so the hand about to reach pulls that side of the body inwards in a sharp 'flick' to initiate the roll.

The discus swing

When you've just done a big move, your trailing hand is now very low and cannot contribute much to the next move from this awkward position. You'll most often find yourself in this position when climbing arêtes or steep juggy routes with big gaps between the holds. In this situation, sometimes it's actually better to remove the trailing hand once you've prepared your feet for the next move, letting it hang in space. Now, draw it back behind you, letting the shoulder follow, as if you were about to throw a discus. Then, swing your shoulder and arm sharply towards the next hold to initiate momentum. It also works for swinging legs towards distant footholds that are far out to the side.

Structure for your understanding

Even the simple act of reading the different types of movement I've just described and grappling with them in your mind is high-value technique training. A key task in learning to understand climbing movement is really engaging the imagination. This process is often described as visualisation. In my opinion, the term isn't up to the job. The visual component is only a fraction of what's needed. 'Seeing' climbing moves is, in fact, more 'feeling' them through your sense of where your body is in physical space. If I asked you to imagine throwing the book you are holding across the room, you could really sense the 'feeling' of your arm drawing back to make space to produce momentum, and you can 'feel' your muscles pull and initiate the movement. The visual part would be imagined as well, but it almost certainly is the less important component. Getting used to linking words in your mind to movements will help these cold descriptions of different movements come alive in your mind and start to work for you. The imagination is your core tool for translating words, images and demonstrations of good climbing technique into understanding; and it needs training too.

Spend some time watching videos of good climbers, looking for each of these movements in action. You'll quickly see that not only are they used on almost every move, but there are countless variations and combinations of them. If you have yet to develop the habit of using momentum and tend to move statically, the best place to start drilling them into your technical repertoire is by practicing each in turn during warm-up or easier boulder problems or sport routes. Even fairly advanced climbers still rarely use all of the above momentum methods habitually. Usually, one or two are lacking and need practiced to develop the habit of automatically selecting them. Identifying which ones are missing is the tricky step. It might become obvious just by visualising your own climbing or sharing feedback with climbing partners. However, gathering some more solid evidence might be needed, such as watching back video of yourself climbing or having a session with a climbing movement coach.

This really is a pivotal component of your technique for moving on rock. Without momentum use, the huge inefficiency of moving statically means that finger strength matters much less that it otherwise would. In other words, it's not really possible to compensate for static movement by focusing on developing strength. Strength is only useful when it can be applied fully. Momentum use gives your strength a huge amount of leverage - you can do much more with a given amount of strength. In this way, it is foundational; it cannot be sidestepped or avoided without placing a ceiling on the effects of training the other performance aspects and thus your overall ability. It would take years of optimal strength training to obtain the same change in climbing ability for a climber who moves very statically as it could be gained in a handful of sessions learning to move with momentum and go much further with the present level of strength. Of course, the idea is to do the strength training, and learn to use it with momentum.

The issue of height

To this day, height is a contentious issue among climbers and is the cause not only of debates about which height is best, but provides a handy excuse for being unable to solve a particular move. The excuse is a false one. Although there is no research available to demonstrate conclusively any patterns of advantage in climbing through height, there is much circumstantial evidence to show that neither extremes of height are a gift for climbers. Obviously, being taller provides an advantage in being able to reach more distant holds, not only at the limit of stretch, but also from a lower position relative to the holds which uses less power. However, this appears to be more than offset (most of the time) by the weight disadvantage that tall climbers have due to body length:volume ratios. So the taller climber is 'unfairly' heavier than the short. The influence of these height and body mass relationships on the difficulty of climbing moves depends to a degree on the nature of the actual move (hold layout, angle etc.), but in general being very tall or small is no great advantage. It may turn out that (other things being equal) being slightly on the short side is very slightly advantageous, but no one can answer that conclusively right now.

Where does leave very tall or very small climbers? It certainly leaves them short of excuses. But that is a good thing. What it does underline once again is the need for momentum. The short cannot reach the holds easily so they will have to move further from the centre of their base of support (i.e. do big moves) much more often. Momentum is the only way to achieve this without needing huge amounts of force from the muscles. The very tall can reach distant holds but often seem to develop a slow moving climbing style. While they rarely cannot reach the holds, hanging onto the poorest ones while reaching with the other hand is often the limiting factor. Their slow, static style works against them on the poor holds. Coaching tall climbers involves spending much time trying to encourage momentum to get their heavy bodies working for them, not against them.

Very tall or very short doesn't appear to matter much in climbing. The issue is how you use momentum to make the most of the advantages your height gives you.

Don't just push with your feet!

The bulk of the potential to improve climbers' movement technique revolves around various ways to get the feet to do more of the hard work of moving the body around in climbing. This can be in use of momentum to allow the lower body to initiate moves, or better understanding of the various forces and the directions in which they operate during moves. Force is not always applied in the downward direction, or on the same angle as the rock and against gravity. During different stages of moves, forces have to be applied in many different directions simultaneously. For example, the hands are not always used for pulling down on holds. Sometimes they might be pulling straight down on an overhead hold, sometimes upwards into an undercut, sometimes pulling directly towards the rock, as in an incut sidepull. It's also not hard to think of hand movements that require pushing away from the rock surface, when palming, mantelshelving or counteracting a 'barn-door'.

When it comes to footwork, climbers are often limited to thinking of the feet as only pushing downwards or in opposition to each other in bridging moves. A major jump of improvement comes when the climber realises that the feet are often pulling as well; and pulling on a large proportion of moves as the rock angle gets steeper.

On overhanging terrain, the feet must pull on the footholds to counteract the tendency of the hips to swing out from the rock. In fact, on most steep moves, the feet must push (to extend the body towards the next hold), and pull (to hold the lower body in and be able to apply the pushing force) at the same time. If you find it hard to imagine how this occurs, try practicing on a single move on a steep board or with feet at the back of a roof. Try the move multiple times and try to notice each separate force in turn.

Feet must also pull the body when they 'lead' the preparation stage of a move. For example a move out left that begins by placing the left foot on a distant foothold well out to the left of the body, while both hands are still on the right. To move the left hand out left, the foot positively pulls the body leftwards, saving the right shoulder from having to work very hard to achieve the same result using the upper body muscles.

Learning this requires noticing the pulling going on from the feet any time you have brain space to pay attention to the components of a move (usually on warm-ups or easier climbs). Also, the more you observe other climbers pulling with the feet, the more you'll build it into your own habits.

A trigger during climbers' development that causes them to fail to learn to pull with the feet and thus climb steep rock, is the angle of the foot placement on footholds. Beginners learning in clunky, insensitive symmetrical rock shoes tend to keep their ankles at a neutral angle on the footholds. The ends of the toes are pointing upwards and not making any contact with the hold. The convex part of the foot at the base of the toes is the part touching the foot hold, but if it's an incut foothold it will be touching the rim of it. So very little surface area is making contact and any significant outward force due to pulling in with the feet causes them to slip and cut loose. So the climber subconsciously learns only to push with the feet.

To 'grab' the foothold and generate enough friction to enable the hips to be

45

pulled in towards the rock and apply more power during moves, the foot placement is crucial. Not just that the foot is placed accurately on the best part of the foothold, but that the toes are pointed down into any incut. Inside the rock shoe, the toes should be actively forcing the shoe to bend into the back of the foothold, with the toes trying to curl in exactly the same way as the fingers grab by curling into the back of the hold. Where the foothold is a rounded, convex shape such as a climbing wall 'blob' shaped hold, the toes should still grab the foothold, but instead of pointing downwards into it, the heel should be lower and foot flatter on the hold. However, the toes should still be trying to wrap closely around the most useful part of the hold, just as the fingers do.

To master steep rock or any situation where the footholds become sparse, the feet must pull too, and pull hard.

Counterintuitive aspects of climbing technique

A large part of climbing can be learned subconsciously, just by doing and not thinking too much, but two aspects of climbing movement stand out as being harder to pick up without consciously noticing and practicing the technique. These are applying maximum possible force to the footholds, and developing body tension on steep rock.

Firstly, applying maximum force to the footholds seems like an odd problem; our bodies are well designed for applying large forces through the lower body. Many sports and other activities require this. We should be used to it. However, in climbing, a common limitation is that climbers are far too passive with the lower body and only really 'try hard' with the upper body. You'll often hear climbers remark that they focused on grabbing and pulling as hard as possible with their hands to complete on a move. But it's rare (apart from elite climbers) to hear them remark that really focusing on delivering maximum power with a foot made the difference between success or failure on a move, but it often does. Why is that?

My hypothesis is that it's down to the coordination challenge of applying maximum force through one or both feet in the moment of a reaching move, while simultaneously achieving the millimetre accuracy to grab the target hold with the hands, and begin to apply force only once the fingers have found the correct spot. It's hard to focus on precision at one end of the body and maximum force at the other. Drummers have exactly the same problem of learning to get hands and feet doing different things simultaneously. Delivering more force through a foot often allows the move to be performed a little slower by taking more share away from the hand that cannot support the body mass on a poor hold while the other reaches. This buys more time to grab the next hold accurately. But it's a learned technique and must be consciously tried, and then practiced to become automatic. There is no shortcutting the conscious, slow, clunky practice of this. At first when you try pulling/pushing super hard with the feet during a dynamic reach, you'll find that the mental energy this takes reduces your accuracy grabbing the handhold. However, over time, the lower body hard work can happen without you having to give it 'processing space'.

Developing and holding body tension, especially (but not exclusively) on steep rock is a related habit that needs a conscious effort to convince the body to adopt. The problem here is that we have to work against an inherent natural tendency of the body to correct it's orientation to vertical in order to find balance. We are simply used to standing and moving in an upright position. It 'feels wrong' to encourage the body to lean backwards during movements. Nevertheless, maintaining contact with footholds out to the side or on steep rock requires us to consciously hold the body in a more horizontal orientation so our hips don't swing away from the foothold. This skill is not so hard when just holding a static position on the rock, or even when moving our feet around. The problem comes when grabbing a hold on a powerful move.

At the moment our hand grabs the next hold, our mind tends to focus completely on the task of first grabbing it accurately and then pulling as hard as possible. It all has to happen in a split second, so a lot of mental energy is needed. That leaves the rest of the body in the hands of the subconscious mind, which does whatever its programmed to do by a combination of natural instincts and training habits. Natural instincts want us to let the hips swing out underneath the newly grabbed hold, to bring our bodies into vertical orientation. It feels 'in balance', but if the feet swing off the footholds and cut loose, this means more force on the handhold. If this doesn't result in a fall on this move, it probably will higher up due to the extra energy used inefficiently.

47

Retraining the subconscious mind to realise that in climbing, sometimes maintaining the horizontal position is not only okay, but essential, is the only way to replace those natural instincts with the ones we need to climb steep rock. Lots of climbers are aware of the importance of body tension and try to train it. The mistake is to concentrate only on building the strength through the body and not the technique. Before extra body strength can be of any use, it's first necessary to teach the body to want to apply body tension subconsciously during hard moves.

Precision really matters

The last two points really underline that you can and should be getting the big muscles of the lower body to do the bulk of the work of holding and moving the body around on rock. The lower body musculature is geared up for this, and once the occasionally counterintuitive movements and forces are learned, it feels so good to let it take the brunt of the force and save your finger strength for the end of the route. However, even though the lower body muscle groups are huge compared to the forearms, the point at which their force is applied to the rock is tiny. The tip of your rockshoes on a small foothold is an even smaller surface area of contact than your fingers taking the same small edge.

So precision does indeed matter. The shape and texture of indoor holds doesn't help us very much in learning foot precision. They are big blobs, protruding from the surface, with good friction anywhere your foot lands. So they tend to shorten the time and mental space you give to looking for the very best part to use. Most of the time that's not a major disadvantage and might be none at all if it's offset by allowing you to move faster up the wall. On some moves however, it will be critical. Indoors this will be on a relatively small proportion of moves. That's not as good as it sounds because it only takes one move on a route that exposes a technical weakness and you've fallen off. Outdoors it's a much bigger problem as many footholds are much smaller or have irregular shapes, with good friction only on one exact spot, such as a sharp crystal. Hence the frustrating and ego destroying time predominantly indoor climbers have moving outdoors, despite often being strong and fit.

There are three options to avoid this problem. If you can do all three, even better. First; climb outdoors a lot, so the body learns to spot the best part of any foothold quickly enough that it doesn't upset your climbing rhythm. Second; if you climb indoors most of the time (even seasonally), make sure you seek out opportunities to restrict your diet of massive blobby footholds. Climb routes with 'feet on features' only, and set boulder problems with limited, small and fiddly footholds that train you to spot and aim for the best spot faster. Third; when failing on a move, blame strength last, not first. It's just as possible you were only relying on strength because your foot wasn't on the right part of the foothold.

Trying to make the hold bigger

When you grab the crux holds of the route, it's easy to think, "Oh no! Is that what I have to pull on?" Climbing, especially onsight does sometimes reward digging deeper to find either a better hold, or a better part of it. This is especially true on real rock when dealing with complex-shaped holds or macro features like tufas. It's human to indulge and overuse this habit of putting off having to pull on a hold that's a lot poorer than you'd like. However, overusing it causes some major knock-on effects with other technical aspects.

Overuse of this delay and adjustment appeals to that part of the mind that likes to put off the pain of progressing through the decisive moment, where success or failure on the climb are most likely to happen. This is especially true when you think the hold might be too poor and you're likely to fail. Obviously, the most likely place you're going to do this is on arrival at the crux. So how does it play out? Some of the time, you'll find something better like openhanding instead of crimping or moving the fingers one centimetre to the side and carry on. Or you'll just waste time. You are hanging on the smallest holds of the entire route, with every second counting as strength is failing, and your searching yields nothing but less energy leftover to actually try the move.

As well as the loss of energy through delay, the other problem is upset of your rhythm. Ideally, you'd take the crux holds and be thinking about nothing but application of maximum strength and precision to get you through the move. Instead, at the very moment you need aggression and pace the most, you must stop and go through the laborious process of conscious move planning and rock reading. Even worse, if you do this enough, it becomes a habit and you stop to feel around more on every route, even when it's really obvious there are no other credible options.

So in the moment of the move, it's a trade off between the efficiency of getting the most out of the rock, and the efficiency of eliminating delay and timing aggression correctly. The longer term effect of slowing down your climbing pace is worth worrying about. Rock reading skill obviously helps here, but what's needed ultimately is a mental cue to remind yourself to try only the most likely options for the best hold position, and then move on before it's too late.

Everyone is a product of their background and the experiences they've been exposed to, unless they've retrained to match their current needs. Worst for overusing this hold searching/adjusting habit are trad climbers who subsequently try to develop their sport climbing or bouldering. They are schooled in off-vertical climbs where time and climbing pace aren't such pressing concerns as precision.

'Board heads' schooled on 45 degree overhanging virtual campusing on blocky pinches have the exactly opposite problem. Their bodies are subconsciously trained through thousands of moves that adjusting tends to lose tension and to just put the feet back on as quickly as possible and dyno to the next hold.

The best climber is the one who has tried both and knows that somewhere in-between wins out in the majority of situations.

Don't overrate strength

Before climbing walls existed, climbers were much weaker. But watching them float up a wave of overhanging french limestone was a beautiful experience. In other words, they really knew how to climb, because they couldn't lean on anything else except perfect technique. Today, the level of strength and fitness among climbers is a mile higher. You'll find two or three teenagers in any city centre climbing wall in the world who are stronger and fitter than most climbing superstars were in the late 1980's. Fitter yes, but they are rarely better athletes.

We tend to value what we can see. Climbing walls offer an excellent resource for getting strong but in some ways a poor resource for getting good at climbing. Before climbing walls, the best climbers aggregated much better - if they had no good climbing where they came from they moved to where the best crags were, with the hardest routes. There, they saw and met the best climbers of the day. This was a great environment for learning technique. They watched the talented trying the same routes, the same moves and copied their technique. And if you didn't understand how they did it, you could just ask them. Informal but priceless technique coaching flowing freely back and forth between climbers.

Climbing walls are full of people climbing with poor technique, and among those climbing the hard routes, a large proportion are the lucky who started off strong and got stronger quickly. There are few good technical examples to learn from, and many examples of the power of being strong and fit. So the young or beginner climber, for whom the climbing wall is 'their world' of climbing to an extent, ends up overvaluing strength and fitness and never seeing the power of good technique enough to go after it, or even realise how far it can take you.

Listening to the message that both technique and strength are needed is, sadly, no match for seeing it first hand. There's nothing like the feeling of someone obviously much weaker than you cruising where you just struggled and fell. Such an experience is priceless for the young and strong. Seek it out.

Bouldering is number one

The most efficient way to get strong for climbing is bouldering. Ask the young, bulky looking lad at the climbing wall who lives under the campus board and he'll tell you differently. He's wrong. He'll tell you that campusing or hanging from a fingerboard, or lifting some weights is more intense and structured so gets you strong quicker. It's not really true. It gets you strong quicker for that activity, so campusers are good at campus boarding. It has power in preparing you for climbing harder only when it's used in proportion to the real climbing.

This is where the campusers go wrong. They boulder, always on their own problems, the same holds, the same angle of board, with the same friends.

51

The character of the moves is the same and the body gets used to it. It ceases to become training. So improvement levels off much quicker than if they had tried a different wall, rock type and asked some other people to show them a problem or two. Frustrated with the lack of strength gain, they turn to campusing as the answer (or other basic strength work). The novelty of this, plus it's intensity is enough to squeeze a bit more improvement out. So they can climb harder problems, with just as limited technique as before.

If you question their rationale for including all this basic strength work, they'll defend it by pointing at the world class climbers who have used basic strength work like the campus board to help them do cutting edge routes. Here's the mistake - those climbers are doing a huge volume and variety of real climbing, with the basic strength work as a supplement. The real climbing moves and hours massively outweigh the campusing. So they have good technique to actually apply the strength edge they get from the campusing.

However, most don't to this. The real climbing hours stay the same or are reduced while the basic strength work hours are added on, sometimes replacing the climbing. The strength gained is more than offset by the losses in technique, and probably the injury time suffered. Basic strength work may seem like a new direction, but when it's replacing real climbing, it's a cul-de-sac.

But I don't like bouldering!

A proportion of climbers just aren't turned on by bouldering. Usually, they've never been shown how to boulder, but it's to be expected that it's not going to appeal to everyone. Yet they still need to get strong for the crux moves of their routes. So bouldering seems like a necessary evil to make gains in strength. Without enjoying it, you can never sustain training long enough to make steady gains over years. So what's the solution?

It's true that it's hard to get strong fingers without the repetitive, maximal pulls on holds that are clocked up in bouldering sessions. So the workaround is to make the most of the one time this actually happens in route climbing: during redpointing. Redpointing routes, especially sport climbs offers the chance to make up the hours repeatedly pulling on small holds.

Even though a proportion of route climbers have such a strong addiction to onsight climbing that they find even this solution hard to stomach; once tried, they can enjoy it as a facet of their climbing. It doesn't need to take over their climbing activity. The reluctance is usually down to ideology rather than actually trying redpoints and failing to get any enjoyment from them. The onsight purists who can't see past onsighting as a worthwhile way to climb will have to see it purely as training (and not admit redpointing is fun, even to themselves), or lean on the fingerboard to get their strength.

How to boulder to show off, or get strong

The social and psychological aspects of climbing walls can be pervasive in completely different directions. For some it can be embarrassment at climbing in public, for others it's showing off. Being the master of your world is a satisfying feeling, as stupid as it sounds. A feeling of mastery in sport is one of the finest goals of sport in general, even if it's just a few square metres of bouldering wall in a dark corner of a climbing centre.

The problem comes when climbers, addicted to this feeling and reluctant to let it go, try to hold onto it by sticking to an ever narrowing field of mastery, either to impress themselves or others at the wall. It seems painful to move on, try something fresh and have to start again from further down the ladder. It's easier to stay comfortable, relive and repeat your best achievements, both publicly and privately.

Of course this approach brings the short term gratification of burning off your friends by milking your knowledge of this board or this hold or rock type. However, it stunts any chance you have of taking your climbing to the next level. To do that, you need the opposite approach. The psychological pattern is the same as the physical one: short term pain for long term results. You must look for the board/angle/move type you are weakest on, and spend two to three sessions on that per one session on in your comfort zone type of climbing.

Boulderers who end up stuck here often see themselves as being ready and willing to seek out their weaknesses and train them. Yet to an outside coach it's obvious that they are simply choosing weaker areas within their strengths. The real weaknesses are not even considered. Even when climbers see this themselves and try to attack it, they still feel the pain of spending time working on areas they genuinely struggle to master. Maybe it's very technical sequences with lots of footwork. Maybe it's steep overhanging ground, or slopers, or endurance routes. The most determined will endure the pain of struggling with it for a good while, but the lure of their comfort zone is always there and it's hard to stay out of it year in year out.

For this commitment to happen, a deeper shift in how you view training has to occur. Those who have got there no longer see true weaknesses as painful, necessary evils that must be endured for a while. They find comfort within them. They view them as an opportunity. Getting to this place is easier said than done. It comes from focusing more on the improvement, and less on the mastery, the result. Focusing solely on the result is enjoyable, but if you indulge it too much, you kill off the capacity to keep producing good results. When both are in balance, maximum enjoyment and improvement happens.

Board heads

The steep bouldering board is the meat and drink of the urban based climber who wants to reach the high grades. At its best it can be the foundation on which huge climbing achievements can be won. At worst, it can be a cul-de-sac at the end of a wasted opportunity to get good at climbing and enjoy the rewards. The difference between the two paths comes down to a set of subtle decisions about how to use it, how not to use it and more generally, how to see it.

The intensity of steep boards is where they earn their value. Their monotony is where they lack value. There is no other way to make so many powerful moves on fingery holds without skin getting too sore. So go ahead and clock up the hours here, but do everything in your power to vary the climbing. Get as many others to set problems as you can. The more varied their body shapes, climbing style and preferences the better. If you can watch them climb their own problems, even better. You'll subconsciously soak up their movement style. Aim not to climb the hardest problem, but every single available problem up to a certain level. Remember that you are training - don't let failure on one specific problem or move dictate your activity on the board, unless it's a move you really are weak on. Change the holds around. You might be able to get away with not doing this for a while if there are plenty of holds, area of board and other problem setters. However, sooner or later, you'll end up getting stronger at climbing only on those moves, on that board, and not for the wider world of climbing.

If you increase the volume of climbing on a single board, make sure the volume of all your other climbing increases too so you gain the technique to actually apply your strength gains from the board. The only exceptions are those climbers who have a home board because there is absolutely no access to any other facility to give some variety. They will have to lean even more heavily on the methods to break up the monotony of the board.

When climbing on the board, don't overuse contrived rules to make the climbing harder such as eliminating sharing hands/feet, heelhooking or other technical solutions. Learn to set better problems instead. It doesn't take long for the techniques you eliminate in training to become eliminated from your habitual repertoire on real rock. Subconsciously, you just don't choose them. If you add or increase the amount of more basic 'system' like problems that train one specific aspect like such as shouldery front-on moves without twisting or dropping the knee, add at least as much practice in these techniques so your body still remembers how to do them.

Overall, be aware that many of the potential benefits of more repetitive, intense training on steep bouldering boards or system boards will be offset by the problems they create elsewhere in your overall game, unless you take steps to minimise this. They are a brilliant tool, used carefully.

A good bouldering session has...

- As much 'shock of the new' as 'Déjà vu'. Do some work on familiar projects, boards, or venues and some work on new ones.

- Delayed gratification. Climb two or three problems on the grip type you are weak on for each one that plays to your strongest grip (this one is not training anything, it's a treat).

- A quick ending to save yourself for tomorrow's session. Two x two hours bouldering in two days is better than one x three hours and then needing a rest day. Obvious in hindsight, hard to actually make yourself do it.

Fingerboard rules

Fingerboards are a good way to supplement finger strength gain in climbing. The first rule of fingerboarding is that it is a supplement. As soon as it's done to replace climbing, it's replacing climbing gains. There are two most common circumstances where it's really useful:

- For those who can only spare enough time to get real climbing done a couple of times a week, but could spare 30 minutes on more days.

- For those who climb a lot and have done so for many years. Their technique has fewer holes and the biggest limitation is stimulating the body aggressively enough to keep getting stronger.

A big resin moulded ugly thing isn't really required. A simple strip of 20mm deep wood, incut but with a skin friendly rounded edge and sanded finish will serve you just as well. In fact it might be more palatable for your relatives who might have to look at it every day on your doorframe. The second rule of fingerboarding is put it somewhere that won't make you lonely or bored stiff. Fingerboard training is short lived, but needs doing regularly, and it's a monotonous business. The main reason for dropout of fingerboarding is sheer boredom. There is one way round this. Put it somewhere you can entertain yourself. For most this will be on the doorframe of their sitting room or kitchen where they can watch TV, listen to music or talk to family and friends. Putting it in a cold dark cellar will feel like punishment, so it won't last. If there's no other option, at least take some music or a laptop and your favourite climbing DVD so you ease the sense of purgatory a little.

Situated correctly, fingerboarding can be a productive addition to fun things you'd be doing anyway like watching TV, chatting or waiting for something to cook. Painless then. If you can stick to it and do it well, it could be the passport to higher grades in time. Quite a lot of time. The big mistake for climbers is to get frustrated and distracted from fingerboarding after the initial improvement of the first few sessions. The forearms are not really cut out for making huge strength gains. They have to be persuaded gently over many years. If you can hang for some more seconds or with more weight than you could last year (not last week!) then you are doing well. The difference and rate of progress seems miniscule when measured on the fingerboard itself. Don't worry too much about this. The difference in your climbing, although still taking months to shine through, could be much bigger.

However, it's all in what you do with them. Fingerboarding will not work for you if:

- You crimp all the time climbing, and add even more crimping on the fingerboard. Your body has got that message already. You need to give it a new one.

- You get injured on it. Good form and listening to the body is critical.

- You don't pull hard enough. Fingerboarding is about applying maximum force, really telling the fingers to hang on harder.

To apply the right force, you need some props for your fingerboard training to help you adjust the force up or down. The problem for many climbers is that hanging with two hands is too easy (i.e. not 100% perceived maximum), but hanging on one hand is way too hard. So you can use props like a book-filled rucksack or a weightbelt (better) to add weight. Or you can go down to one hand and use props to remove body weight such as a foot on a correctly positioned chair, a hanging sling, a hanging set of scales to hold onto or something else you can use as a poor hold for the free hand. A poor supporting hold might be one or two fingers of the other hand on the fingerboard, or low down on the doorframe, or a light switch box or something. Be inventive and find props that work for you.

A good fingerboard session

If you only have a finger edge rung, you could start with a few sets of two handed hangs. Always hang on the fingerboard with a bent arm. If you do a lot of fingerboarding from a straight arm, it's a common cause of various forms of elbow tendinitis. After this, you can progress to some sets of pull ups, then slightly harder deadhangs until you feel comfortable and ready to pull with full power. How long the warm-up takes depends on your body and the progression of the warm-up. Some will be ready for the hard sets after five or ten minutes. For some it will be more.

The workout is given structure by the grip types you want to train. The grip types are crimped (often half-crimped on the fingerboard as it feels less aggressive on the joints), openhanded with four fingers and openhanded with three fingers. Three fingers openhanded grip translates well to two finger pockets and mono pockets, but if you are training to do routes with a lot of hard pocket moves, you could do some hangs on these too, carefully. Using less than three fingers on the fingerboard is always more aggressive and harder on the finger joints. When several fingers are used, they support each other and provide more rotational stability. Fingerboarding with two or less fingers is a quick way to get inflamed PIP joints or even collateral ligament damage if form is not perfect and you don't know when to back off.

Simply performing a few sets on each hand, on each grip type you are going to train is your workout. As hinted above, the makeup of this is determined by your weaknesses. Test them on a set deadhang. Find an arrangement that feels close enough to maximum force so that you can only manage to hang on for 5-8 seconds before failure. For many this will be on one hand with some assistance from the other hand on a sling or other support. Compare the maximum length of your hang with each grip type. Whichever you are weakest on will be what you should do most of. Persist until your maximum strength is equal across all the grip types, and once you've achieved that you can train them all equally. This will probably take many months or even years.

Alternatively, you could use the fingerboard as a tool to bootstrap your way out of a really bad grip type weakness. Commonly, this will be an extreme over reliance on crimping. Most climbers keep crimping nearly everything until the inevitable pulley injuries forces them to do otherwise. Yet climbing openhanded feels so completely alien that they struggle to break the habit or even see how they could pull on holds with an openhanded grip. For them, doing solely openhanded work on the fingerboard might be a good answer. Working it in isolation from whole climbing moves will help gain familiarity with it and gain some steps up the strength ladder enough that they realise that openhanded works on real holds, and works well!

The deadhang should be hard enough so that it takes a real effort and concentration to manage, holding the hang as long as possible until your bent arm starts to drop. At failure point, let your feet come back down to the floor rather than letting your fingers open and rip off the hold. If you could only hang for two or three seconds, it was a little too hard and the hang time was too short to provide a decent stimulus for the muscles. If it was getting up towards ten seconds, it's starting to get too easy and you need to change the conditions to make it harder and shorten the hang time by a couple of seconds. You'll need to be inventive with your props and willing to experiment to get it right. You'll also need to be flexible, because seemingly imperceptible changes in your recovery state, skin wear or the temperature and humidity of the room could mean you can't touch what was easy for you last time. Don't get hung up about this, just adjust the difficulty of the hang and carry on. Resting about a minute between sets (on the same hand) should be enough. If you can consistently use less rest than this without performance level dropping, you are probably not applying enough effort on each set. How many sets you do on each grip type depends completely on your recovery from other climbing sessions and your stage of development among many components. Let your body decide. If you are failing to maintain strength through the session and each set is feeling weaker than the last, you should have stopped already. Experiment and stick with a given volume for a week or so and then try upping the volume a bit until you nudge up against that limit where fatigue starts to interfere with completing sessions. Pull back a touch from this, continue for a few weeks and then try again.

Since the fingers are placed under maximal load repeatedly, perfect form is critical to make fingerboarding safe. When form is perfected, the exercise is very controlled and it can feel safer for the fingers than normal climbing. Centre the body under the fingerboard before pulling off the ground to prevent any swinging. If you do find yourself swinging, stop the set, re-position and start again. Make sure the fingertips are well chalked for each set. Sweaty fingers cause a risk of slight slips under load which can cause pulley tears. A common error made by beginners is to make a little jump off the ground when initiating the hang, in anticipation of it being hard. This seems to be an intuitive thing to do, but the result is a shock load on the fingers which again is dangerous. Instead, pull steadily harder with the fingers until you pull your feet off the ground into a hang underneath a bent arm.

If you are climbing two or three times per week at a reasonably high level,

59

you might be able to handle another 1-3 fingerboarding sessions on the other days of about 30-40 minutes in length including the warm-up. This would allow you to do some valuable training on days then you don't have time to get to the climbing wall. The fingerboard session could even happen before work or during lunch for the motivated and busy. Those climbing more than three times per week will have to be more careful to see if they are ready to add supplementary training. It could either be done at home on what would previously have been rest days, or included on the climbing days right after the warm-up.

The longer term

It takes time for the gains of fingerboarding to become obvious. You should notice an increase in your basic level of finger strength as months go by. Since this is strength gained in isolation from your climbing technique, your body will take extra time to learn how to apply the extra strength. So if you have a had a spell of heavy training with gains showing during the training, don't be disheartened if you go back out on real rock and the difference isn't as immediate as you hoped. Give it a month or so of climbing on the real stuff to get a clearer idea of whether it's working.

Errors in form, or ignoring messages from the body about recovery state are common in fingerboarding. Climbers get into a routine and stick to it no matter what - despite tiredness, poor conditions or aches and pains that develop slowly. It's good to keep training hard, but maintenance of effort doesn't mean you shouldn't be flexible and just do the climbing or rest for a week if something isn't right. Injuries do happen too, developing from poor form or training when tired or mentally preoccupied. It's a shame, because getting form right in fingerboarding is quite simple. Sometimes, a niggling injury can be started during climbing, and developed into something worse by the intensity of fingerboarding. Don't be afraid to just stop it altogether. If you've already been doing it for a while you'll have made some good gains and you can come back to it after a few months or more of just climbing. Flexibility, and not getting stuck or emotionally attached to one routine of training is the way to stay healthy.

To crimp or not to crimp

Crimp to get strong on crimps, but crimp with care!

There is a common discussion about the wisdom of crimping during training. Crimping is the riskiest grip position for the fingers. The more systematic your training of it, the risk of picking up a pulley injury, or just inflamed and swollen PIP joints gets really high. However, there's no getting away from the fact that the best climber is the one who is equally strong in all the different grip positions.

Making sure you are strong in different grips, but avoiding finger injuries is a fine balance to achieve. There are quite a few variables to steer through to minimise injury risks and get the best possible strength gains.

In my experience, crimping is needed to get strong at crimping. So the idea that some support that you can avoid it altogether and still get strong on crimps I feel is incorrect. The limited research available supports that you must train particular positions to make optimal strength gains in them. Some high profile climbers have disagreed with this, feeling that it has been possible for them to train openhanded, yet still achieve a high level of crimp strength and avoid injury. Their methods are undoubtedly a step forward, but their own analysis of them has a couple of major problems.

First of all, there is a definition problem with crimping. A full crimp with the thumb over the index finger seems to be the hardest on the body. We use them a lot on real rock, but not so much when training indoors. Climbers doing a lot of systematic bouldering on steep indoor boards are often pinching fingery, blocky holds. They may consider this not to be crimping, but the PIP (middle) joint of the fingers is flexed and is essentially a half crimp position. Climbers have chosen this setup of steep boards because it trains the whole body for climbing very efficiently. The side effect of this is that even the fingery holds are slightly bigger than outdoors and tend to be pinched due to the blocky nature of bolt-on holds. This pinch position ends up being used very commonly and will translate well to crimping. But the slightly larger holds and less acute angle of the PIP joint seems to allow more training to happen with fewer injuries. Secondly, those climbers training a lot indoors are then 'performing' outdoors using a full crimp often. They might not count this as part of the training, but it is.

Crimping on boulder problems can be much safer than crimping on a fingerboard or especially a campus board. Few climbers crimp on the campus board for long without injury - the forces peak so rapidly on the sudden dynamic movements that it gets really dangerous. Crimping on the fingerboard can be quite safe if your form is perfect. And crimping without the thumb helps to make the position more natural when using one hand or two hands quite close together.

The safest formula will be to do the most intensive basic strength work with a four or three finger openhanded grip, and train crimps mostly on steep powerful boulder problems. That said, any crimping is only relatively safe if your technique is good. Poor footwork, leading to sudden foot slips, or a violent climbing style will make it just as dangerous as campusing. Crimping during real climbing tends to be less hard on the body because the accelerations are slower than with campusing. Also, the body is often turned underneath the hold to bring the wrist into a neutral position during the highest force part of the move and the hold is generally grabbed openhanded before closing into a crimp.

Having said all this, the vast majority of climbers crimp far too much and would seriously benefit, in both performance and injury risk, in developing their openhanded grip to a point where they use it more often than crimps and are at least as strong openhanded as crimped.

Mini case study: I used to be one of those who crimped too much, and averaged about 3 serious pulley injuries per year for 5 years until I finally was forced to get strong openhanded, and to love this grip position too. Since then I've had one very minor pulley tweak (needing only a slight drop in training intensity for a few weeks) in the past five years.

Making sense of Haston and Oddo

One of the most striking trends in elite level sport climbing in the last couple of years has been the age of the top performers. In many other sports, personal best performances at a world class level happen during the twenties and early thirties. The reasons for this are actually quite complex and have a lot to do with the limitations on performance set by other sports. It's also heavily dependent on how much the sport relies on particular performance aspects. For instance, sports heavily reliant on pure strength, endurance or reaction time are harder to perform in for either the very young or old.

However, sports more reliant on technique or with a broader range of contributing skills make age slightly less important. It seems climbing is one of these sports. Climbing is a slightly unusual case because of its unstructured freedom. There is immense opportunity to find a niche within its broad church of activities in which you can excel. This can take a long time to discover. So for lots of reasons, climbers can be good at a very young or impressively old age. It seems every year that goes by sees the highest grades in climbing (especially sport climbing) achieved by both younger and older extremes. At the time of writing this book, we have French Enzo Oddo climbing several 9as at 14, and Stevie Haston climbing his first 9a at 52. A related phenomenon is the small difference between elite performances between men and women.

The short message here is that it's never too early or late to get a lot better at climbing and there are few excuses available. What common elements can we see from these extremes of young and old performers that give us clues on what to focus on? Perhaps the first thing to say is not to underestimate the experience of the young. Many of the best teenage climbers operating at 8c+ or harder in sport climbing began at age 5 or younger and live in continental countries with a nearly endless resource of nearby sport crags. They are the first generation to benefit from this. They were often introduced to the sport through parents who are also regular sport climbers, so the conditions are there to clock up a staggering volume of climbing in a short time. The influences of these climbers are nearly perfect. Coached by expert parents and surrounded by a peer group that is unerringly positive and centred around good performance, they learn and engrain good habits from day one. So their progression will be much faster than most others could dream of.

The old climbers of this generation didn't have such a great start. They learned while climbers were still in the early days of figuring out how to get really good at climbing. Everything was hit and miss: the knowledge, the influences and the tactics. The abundance of sport climbing has helped them too - more moves per year, less horrible routes, bad indoor climbing holds that cause injuries and better diet. The old have had their fair share of injuries. In other sports, they might have kept trying to compete every year, and made those injuries worse until they ended the game. But climbers know their dream climbs will still be there in a few years. They can afford to wait, try some other climbing styles for a while and recover at the pace the body dictates, not the competition schedule. So they recover to fight another day. It's not too late.

The messages from this:

- Start climbing early and move to somewhere with a LOT of climbing and good climbers.

- Sport climbing is less reliant on brute strength and more on technique. It's easier to be good at a young or old age.

- Climbing is flexible. Train your weaknesses but play to your strengths, choose routes that suit you to make your personal bests.

- Go at the pace of your body. You have time to absorb injuries and still get better.

Making sense of Ondra and Sharma shapes

Pretty early on in the history of rock climbing, climbers deduced that body mass ought to be, and is an important element of performance. So began a series of generations of climbers who've starved their way to hard grades, or suffered the pain of a constant battle to be lighter. Hope for climbers with big bodies or big appetites comes in the shape of famous exceptions to the 'less is more' rule for body mass in climbing: big successful climbers. They just didn't fit the picture (at first glance). They were heavy, even fat, yet still seemed able to compete with the wiry. Perhaps being heavy but strong could match light but weak? To this day, the confusion and argument rumbles on, and more exceptions keep popping up to reignite the issue.

Maybe the most famous and illuminating 'fat but fit' example was John Dunne in the late eighties and early nineties. Climbing 8c+ when only a handful in the world had, while eating as much as the rest of the 8c+ climbers put together. It didn't really make sense. So much so they even doubted his honesty. How did he do it? First of all, it's necessary to study his case in the context of the day. Whether it was deliberate or not, it seems that John was one of the first climbers to take advantage of periodisation. When spotted at the crag (he was obvious from some distance), he was notably unfit and seemed a mile off the level his achievements suggested. Yet others would testify to his amazing fitness and prowess when he was on form. He was maybe the first to adopt the routine of training heavy, performing light. John was not naturally built for rock climbing. He would be better suited to moving large rocks rather than moving on them. So to succeed he'd not worry about his weight until he was getting ready for projects, then drop 30-40 pounds (reputedly) to 'peak' for a short time.

Other giant exceptions from this period were Stevie Haston who "could bicep curl a small sport climber" but weighed as much as two of them, and Fred Nicole whose forearms look as heavy as most sport climbers' thighs. Perhaps these two climbers provide a clue to the success of perhaps the most famous exception: Chris Sharma.

Making inferences about the distribution of muscle around the body by casual observation is a shaky path, but in the absence of any research on climbers in this area, it at least provides some circumstantial evidence that makes more sense of the body types we see doing well in climbing. Looking at Sharma, Nicole, Dunne and any other climber who has reached a really high level in a heavy body, we can see something common: more of the weight than normal is in the upper body. In more formal language, they have an unusual somatotype. Their large upper bodies are well built to handle the volumes of climbing necessary to get really good without the upper body becoming overworked and getting injured as much. More climbing can be done in a given space of time, so more technical learning can happen, in addition to the building of more muscle in the places that are normally limiting for climbers. This is not to say they don't have to work as hard, it's just that they have a great starting place to learn to climb well and deal with training. It's also probably only a very small advantage, only noticeable because these few outstanding athletes have all the other attributes and habits that allow them to take advantage of it.

So what about the majority, who have large thighs, and small forearms. First of all, it would be better if they started to climb when they were kids and still had small thighs and forearms, and the development of muscle would be a little different. But if it's too late for that, it's still not too late to make big changes. Muscle is a plastic tissue. It diminishes when not used, and grows when used vigourously. Muscle distribution will gradually shift towards the upper body when the stimulus (lots of climbing instead of running, cycling etc) demands this.

Be clear on the lesson from the details of the big exceptions in climbing. Being light still matters. There are far more skinny Adam Ondras than chunky Chris Sharmas doing well in rock climbing and that is not an accident. Climbers who look more like Adam Ondra (stick thin) to start with will do well when they can put on as much muscle in the upper body by powerful climbing as they can. Those who start off with John Dunne legs but not arms will do well by getting lighter, but not so much that they cannot manage hard powerful bouldering week in, week out, and that requires some fuel.

The final lesson from the big exceptions is the time it took for them to look like they do. Most of the best climbers in the world have a background of fifteen to twenty years climbing and very few have less than ten. When climbers with some weight to lose try to do something about it, they want to make a nearly overnight transformation by comparison. It takes time to change the shape of your body without causing more problems than you solve. So take your time.

How light do I need to be?

It's clear that strength to weight ratio is very important in climbing, and there's very few climbers around who wouldn't benefit from prioritising a change in some aspect that contributes to it. Nevertheless, a little more detail is needed to get a clear picture of what a good climbing-specific strength to weight ratio means.

Taking the strength side of the ratio first, the area of the body that requires the most work to gain strength is the fingers. However, the whole upper body musculature needs to be strong enough to manoeuvre the body around in awkward or extreme positions which requires a lot of force. The amount of muscle required in the upper body depends on the weight of the rest of the body. Ideally, if the lower body is not so well developed, the upper body needn't be either. So the whole climber is lighter. On the most brutally powerful of moves, it can be a disadvantage not to have enough muscle, but this is more than outweighed by the advantage of being light if the climber wants to be good at routes. More muscle is not such a huge disadvantage on very short routes and in bouldering, but carrying big heavy muscles a long way up a cliff, when all of their firepower is only occasionally needed is inefficient.

The weight part of the ratio needs to be seen as two separate issues - lean mass (muscle) and fat. Lots of climbers would benefit from having less of both. In fact, often a lot less. However, there are some complicating issues because of the interdependence of the different facets of performance in climbing. The effect of shedding, for example, 5kg of excess body fat on climbing ability is not a fixed quantity that will be similar for any climber. Several things could make the size of the effect radically different. First, the effect of shedding weight will be much greater if the climber has good technique. It will also be greater for a stronger, fitter climber. The more weight stands out as a critical weakness in the climber's game, the bigger the effect of shedding excess weight will have.

There are a significant proportion of climbers who have the opposite problem - they have a naturally very light frame and low body fat percentage, apparently no matter what they eat. They have a great base to start from in climbing, but a big challenge too. Their challenge is to be able to make significant gains in muscle to manage the really powerful moves. Many of them never manage it because they avoid their opportunities to. Many lighter-built climbers gravitate towards what they are inevitably most suited for - long fingery endurance climbs. That is fine of course, but even for these climbs, attacking the really steep powerful boulder problems and routes will help gain enough muscle to deal with more powerful moves.

So what exactly is a good weight for climbing? Of course I cannot answer that numerically! I can only say that the ideal body composition for climbing is as low as possible body fat percentage (that can be managed safely and comfortably in conjunction with a hard physical sport), a fairly small lower body muscle mass and a small but significant upper body muscle mass.

Whether climbers should consider manipulating their weight depends on the starting weight, muscle mass, body fat, age, gender and the climbing goals. Ignoring any one of these factors will lead to making poor choices with regards to aiming for the right weight, with serious negative consequences.

A significant proportion of world class climbers maintain exceptionally low body fat percentages for large parts of the year (but rarely indefinitely). For males this might be around 4% and for females 10-12%. Most climbers would really struggle to maintain this without running into health problems related to nutrition without professional supervision. 8-10% for males and around 22% for females is a more realistic ideal fat percentage. 3% body fat in males and 12% in females is essential for normal physiological function of the body.

Maintaining a really low body fat can have serious health implications for either sex, but it is an especially pertinent issue for females, whose safe lower limit of body fat varies dramatically from person to person. Menstrual dysfunction (amenorrhoea) is caused by the physiological stress of reducing body fat stores too far, and leads to bone loss and other serious health problems. 40% of females of reproductive age participating in regular sporting activity suffer from amenorrhea, compared to 2-5% in the general population. The first signs of this are irregular menses (oligomenorrhoea). The symptoms can usually be reversed by increasing energy intake a little, giving resumption of the menstrual cycle. However, chronic calorie restriction of over three years has been shown to cause irreversible bone loss (osteoporosis) in distance runners. Increasing body fat to 17% is thought to be a critical level for onset of menstruation and 22% to ensure normal menstrual cycles. The variation in the safe lower body fat limit for females is due to the additional contribution of various factors such as genetics, nutrition, additional stress and lifestyle factors. Hence, there are many female athletes who sustain a body fat percentage under the critical 17% level without menstrual dysfunction.

The risks of manipulating body fat to low levels are also severe for children and youth climbers, who risk stunting their growth and interfering with the development of their bodies and causing a series of other developmental negative effects. Quite apart from the associated health problems, these effects end up being completely counterproductive for your climbing.

The correct attitude to have to weight and climbing is to keep a sense of perspective and develop a keen ear for the messages from the body as you grow and progress as a climber at whatever level. Young climbers need the long term advantages of being able to develop strong and healthy tendons and build muscle tissue far more than they need the short term advantage of making a weight that requires constant attention to maintain. Those that restrict eating chronically at an early age pay for it later with injury and limited potential to develop to a really high level. Excess weight is extremely rarely the overriding weakness for female climbers. If any weight manipulation is needed, it's more often gain in upper body muscle mass from powerful climbing that would help. Normally, the effect of changes in body mass for females are completely masked by the much more common and larger weaknesses of fear of falling and its consequences for technical efficiency.

The most common group among climbers who would benefit from losing weight tend to be male climbers in their 20's and beyond. Body fat percentage is often at 20% or more and would benefit from a modest reduction. Even for those who have a low body fat percentage, involvement in other 'lower body sports' (e.g. cycling) results in a high muscle mass in the lower body. This starts to limit development increasingly at the upper grades in climbing. Some careful weight reduction can help to add more leverage to the other performance aspects. For a handful of climbers out there who are elite in most performance aspects, it may even be the final piece of the jigsaw puzzle that opens the door to the top level. For this group, educating themselves in sound, scientifically based sports nutritional practice (beyond the scope of this book) will allow them to walk this risky line between a real performance edge and a dangerous and counterproductive obsession.

How to get light without pain?

The basic elements of losing body mass for sport are relatively simple. Yet it causes more headaches and confusion than maybe any other performance aspect in climbing. At its foundation is the energy balance equation: if 'calories in' falls short of 'calories out', the athlete will lose weight. But everyone knows the reality of weight loss is a much more complex picture of interactions of different factors that influence our calorie consuming and expending habits. Navigating this minefield is made harder still by the constant distraction of unscientific and poorly thought out diet books churned out by the weight control industry, driven by profit, not by motivation to help you.

A thorough discussion of this subject is beyond the scope of this book (I am preparing a dedicated title for climbers shortly after this book). However, I have outlined some of the main tenets of successful weight loss for climbers (athletes) below.

Simply eating a healthy 'athlete's diet' together with maximising physical activity to use more energy is the single best method to achieve and maintain a low body fat percentage. The 'athlete's diet' differs slightly from a recommended diet for non-training situations in two main aspects. First, a higher proportion of carbohydrate is needed, and second, the timing of meals becomes important to improve the rate and quality of recovery from training.

Making sense of the popular diets

Lots of climbers have experimented with the multitude of famous 'branded' dieting methods sold to you via books or subscriptions. The best known examples include the Atkins diet which recommends drastically reducing carbohydrate intake, or the GI diet which recommends use of particular types of carbohydrate to reduce appetite. These dieting ideas tend to propose a mechanism that revolves around a complicated aspect of human metabolism or the chemical makeup of the foods we eat. Some of these mechanisms can be quite valid, even proven by good quality research. However, the suggested mechanism (designed to make you believe that this diet will be more successful than another) is probably not the primary mechanism that contributes to any weight loss experienced. This is down to the diet plans causing you to tip the energy balance - i.e. eating less calories, or using more through activity.

In this way, elements of what these popular diets recommend can be useful or even essential tools for some to lose weight in the short term. In the longer term however, many of these diets are extremely unsuccessful in helping dieters hold on to their lower weight. This is especially true when they recommend eliminating whole food groups or combining foods in unappealing or socially inconvenient ways. What's more, this is not necessary.

The evidence shows that successful long term weight control is most likely when a handful of components are used in combination. These include:

- Increasing activity.

- Gentle moderation of portions and treats, applied with flexible restraint.

- Slow weight loss with modest, achievable goals.

- Varied, healthy diet with plenty of low energy density foods (mainly fruit and veg).

- Use of additional techniques to take attention away from appetite.

Using only one or two of these components in isolation makes it much harder to succeed at weight control. At the very least, it will delay success and make the process more painful for those who wish to lose weight.

Steps for weight management in climbing

The first stage that determines whether you can stick to a plan to lose weight or fail mid way through (as most do) is to underpin the motivation to do it in the first place. If you are overweight for climbing, the effect of correcting this is likely to be large. It will be highest if the other areas of your performance are already well developed. For people in this situation, it can be a plateau breaker. Measure your body fat percentage as accurately as you can. Your local fitness gym, school, university or even leisure centre will be good places to track down a set of skin-fold calipers and someone who can tell you how to use them. The next best thing to estimate body fat percentage is a bio-impedance device. Even the good quality ones are likely to have an error range up to about 5% either side of the true figure, which means you should never use them as anything more than a very rough guide. For instance, if you are male and the device suggests your body fat percentage is 20-25% then it will give you useful data that losing some weight is likely to help your climbing. If it returns a low figure like 9%, it would not be a good idea to use this data alone to decide to lose any weight. First get more reliable data from calipers with the correct algorithm for calculating the result.

The really tough decision is for those climbers whose body fat percentage and general body mass is already fairly low. Would that extra kilo lost give you the edge you need to secure those dream climbing goals? Perhaps. However, inevitably there will be a point where the benefits of being lighter will be outweighed by problems recovering from training due to underfeeding or poor nutritional content of the diet. Maintaining a weight that is so low it is difficult to sustain without severe calorie restriction is quite likely to lead to problems with motivation when good climbing performances become directly dependent on your appetite control. This sort of situation is ripe for development of disordered eating in a minority. Like any other aspect of training, going too far with it brings greatly diminished and eventually negative results.

Many training advice books and articles are reluctant even to discuss body mass optimisation for climbers head on. The general recommendation is not to worry about weight at all, because of the dangers of complications of aggressive weight loss. My take is that this approach won't really work. I don't think it's realistic to think that generations of young, psyched climbers who are determined to improve as fast as they can will ignore that the elite climbers they see and adopt as role models tend to be light. It's inevitable that some will experiment, or at the very least feel pressure to get lighter themselves. Young climbers, who are still developing are one group who definitely should avoid getting to low body fat percentages, to protect their health and longer term development into adult climbing athletes. But adult climbers will frequently benefit from experimenting carefully with modest weight reduction.

Dealing with the question of weight head on by measuring current body fat percentage, and monitoring it as it changes, will help inform the process. It should in fact reduce the numbers of climbers who develop disordered eating through ignorance about whether weight manipulation is actually a good idea for them.

Measure fat percentage. If it's already very low, look elsewhere in the big picture of climbing improvement to find gains. If it could be lower, set a modest goal and assess the effect it had on your climbing and your basic strength-weight ratio. It really helps to have a standard way of measuring you can keep coming back to over time, such as a boulder problem or fingerboard deadhang set that is near your limit. Remember not to measure the effectiveness of the diet during a calorie restricted phase of dieting. The data will be useless because the body will be lighter due to low glycogen and water stores during the diet. Wait until you are normally carbo-loaded before measuring results.

A modest goal for a male climber of average height and 25% body fat might be 2kg in the medium term. At 10% or below it would be 0.5kg. Take each modest goal as it comes and assess the results diligently. Was it hard to achieve the weight loss? Was it hard to maintain the new weight without continued dieting? Did it have a positive effect on the climbing? Notice any potentially significant things that happened during the process such as feeling tired, unable to complete your normal volume of climbing, mood changes, developing injuries, menstrual disruption or anything else unusual. Any of these are possible messages that either the weight loss is too much, too fast or poorly executed. The safest thing to do if you run into these sorts of problems is stop dieting and begin eating a normal volume of healthy food that's enough to maintain your current weight or even gain a little again. If you are sure that your fat percentage is not too low and the strategy of the weight loss is the problem, take the time to educate yourself in successful sports nutrition strategies either by reading dedicated texts on weight optimisation and nutrition for sport, or seeking some professional advice from a sports nutritionist. Access might not be too expensive through a local gym or sports medicine clinic.

Once you've set an appropriate goal for the weight loss, take time to devise a strategy to best achieve it. You are most likely to succeed when calorie restriction is matched by increase in activity. Climbers commonly turn to running, cycling or other cardiovascular (CV) exercises to achieve weight loss this way. There is nothing wrong with these and introducing some CV exercise is good for your general long term health (although there are rarely substantial direct ergogenic effects for rock climbers). However, they are not the most efficient or effective forms of calorie burning exercise that could be done for climbers. Actually, more climbing is likely to be much better overall. The main exception is where you are already doing about as much climbing as your body can handle (a tiny minority). The rationale for cardiovascular exercise to burn calories is that it uses large muscle groups continuously over a long period. Yet climbing endurance training; doing repeated pumpy routes or circuits uses energy at comparable rates. Climbing endurance training tends to have an aerobic and anaerobic component. Anaerobic training is short lived compared to aerobic training but burns calories vastly higher rate. Burning calories with more climbing instead of some other non-specific activity has the obvious plus point of improving both your climbing specific endurance and technique at the same time. So unless you are doing a huge volume of climbing training per week already, this is likely to be a better use of your time.

When it comes to the calorie intake side of the energy equation, the first priority is to look for unhealthy dietary habits you can replace. Replacement of consistently consumed 'bad' foods that are high in fat or very energy dense is the easiest way to increase the likelihood of weight loss success. It's usually alcohol, fried food, fatty food, indulgence in confectionary or very frequent and systematic elements of the diet like sugar or full fat milk in tea or coffee that are the easy targets. For plenty of us, just picking one of these habits to replace would be enough to lose weight without doing anything else. However, making some modest, palatable changes in several at once makes it less painful. Which you choose obviously depends on your personal preferences. For some, the simplicity of eliminating fully one single bad food habit, like chocolate or sugar in tea is the easiest to manage and stick to. If you need to make quite substantial changes to your diet, or restrict elements that you find painful to do (like alcohol, or fried food), then the research shows that flexible restraint (allowing limited but regular treats) is much more successful than complete abstinence.

The biggest fear of the dieter is their own appetite and the thought of feeling constantly hungry. Any diet, whether to lose or maintain a given weight that leaves you feeling deprived of food is unsustainable in the long term (probably the short term too). It's also unnecessary unless you are attempting to gain an unrealistically low weight. The maximum rate of weight loss that tends to be successful in the longer term is about 0.5kg per week. This equates to a roughly 500 calorie deficit per day. Increasing the volume of low energy-density foods in your diet, and especially using these to replace higher energy-density foods helps to achieve a calorie deficit without too much effect on appetite. Searching the internet will bring plenty of examples of good low energy foods that fit your preferences. Thankfully, most fruit and vegetables fit this category. Eating fruit and vegetables as snacks is not only excellent nutritional practice but is a fantastic diet-aid. Drinking water or other low calorie drinks is also very useful for controlling appetite.

Unfortunately, dieting while maintaining a demanding routine of exercise/ training has some extra concerns that are important to get right. First of all, it's important to make sure that restricting your calorie intake during weight loss or permanent dietary habit changes doesn't decrease the variety and therefore nutritional quality of your diet. Again, a detailed discussion of the potential pitfalls is beyond the scope of this book and a good sports nutrition text should be your guide. However, there is a critical role of carbohydrate in recovery that really needs mentioning here.

Good recovery from climbing sessions is a multifaceted process, but often the rate limiting component is replacement of the muscle fuel store (glycogen). Failure to replenish the glycogen store often accounts for that wasted feeling you get when you have trained on consecutive days until you have a session where it's impossible to summon strength that would have been easy for you just days ago. Your ability goes off a cliff within an hour of starting the session: the tank is empty. Muscle glycogen provides the bulk of the fuel needs for exercising muscles. So recovery is partly determined by the rate of glycogen replenishment in muscle. This is not a fixed quantity. There is a special 'golden window' right after the glycogen has been used where glycogen replenishment runs much faster. This window, which lasts around two hours after the session is caused by changes in the hormonal conditions that encourage rapid uptake of glucose from the bloodstream. Anyone that wants to make large and regular demands of their glycogen store (i.e. train hard and as regularly as possible) needs to take advantage of this feature of our metabolism. This means a steady supply of glucose in the blood right after you climb, in the form of a carbohydrate rich meal. The ideal post training meal consists of some high GI index carbs such as bread or other sugary foods as well as some lower GI foods that take a little longer to digest and spread out the supply of blood glucose across the two hour window.

It follows that it's important to eat as soon as possible after the session. In fact if you have any travelling to do to get home, it's a good plan to start off the supply by eating a carb rich snack as soon as you finish climbing. On a separate note, a carb rich meal right after training also offsets a large dip in immune function that occurs immediately after training. Without this, you are much more vulnerable to catching colds, flus and more serious illnesses in this post training window. This is why you tend to catch illnesses when particularly tired or worn down from heavy training plus other stresses.

Those trying to lose weight should make sure they still fuel up before and immediately after their sessions to minimise the energy and nutrient shortfall affecting their recovery from climbing so much. It is well after the post training meal and especially during periods or days when less activity is going on (like rest days) that the most moderation of calorie intake should take place. Whether losing or maintaining weight, the athlete's diet should have a slightly higher proportion of carbohydrate than that of a sedentary person. 60-70% of calories coming from carbohydrate is the correct range to aim for. This is actually harder than it might seem with a typical western diet, which often contains much too high a proportion of dietary calories coming from fat.

The notes above are just the headlines. If you are planning to manipulate your weight for climbing, especially to low levels of body fat, I'd recommend more dedicated reading or a professional consultation. It will be money well spent to avoid the dieting travails of the 90% or so dieters who fail to maintain their target weight in the long term.

Who needs to pump iron to climb hard?

The biggest problem with weightlifting in training is the effect it has on people. When used correctly, it is a useful tool and a solution to various training problems, even in climbing. However, those who use it at all frequently over use it and choose their exercises poorly on top of this. So the net result is that weight training hinders climbing performance nearly as often as it helps it. Perhaps its simplicity, measurability and convenience is part of why it seems to be so addictive for some.

In general, weight training is not really the most efficient form of training for the vast majority of climbers. Nearly all climbers need to climb more. So they should spend any spare time they have for training just doing the climbing related stuff. Weight training is a powerful but rather blunt instrument, even when done correctly. For climbers who have other things in their lives besides climbing (so their time for training is limited), some other form of real climbing is always a more time efficient way to make gains. It's possible to target specific muscle groups or areas of weakness in climbing in just the same way as weight training, but still be learning technique and tactics at the same time. Time spent pumping iron is time not learning any climbing skills.

The two main situations where weight training can be a good idea follow directly from this point; when the climber is so advanced and doing so much climbing, they need the pure intensity offered by basic strength training. Or, when circumstances (usually work) take you away from any opportunity to climb for long periods; no technique learning is possible, and the weights are just a means to make whatever gains are possible instead of lose strength. Weights can also be of use for some other exceptional cases such as recovery from injury or to build a foundation of body strength for those who struggle with moving over steep ground at all because of lack of significant muscle mass. Let's look at these in turn.

The Pro

A handful of elite climbers use weight training to supplement their climbing training. However, a majority of their peers do not and can still perform well or better. So there is no clear evidence that it offers an advantage. There are only the testimonies of the climbers themselves. Such surmising is poor evidence for making wider assumptions. Climbers at elite level need a large, intense training stimulus, and variety in the training modality used to keep the body responding and break plateaus. Weights could be used as a 'shock to the system' to provide a fresh stimulus for a relatively short time, or when there is so much climbing in the climber's program that adding more wouldn't be practical and a very intense stimulus will maintain strength gains in conjunction with a lot of endurance training. Another advantage of weights in this case is that it allows more body strength training to happen than the fingers might allow. Very large amounts of hard bouldering will be hard on finger skin, PIP joints and finger flexor tendons and pulleys. It may also be useful for preparing for a specific move that requires extreme body strength and is less limited by finger strength, such as very powerful or overhanging moves.

Choosing the exercises will obviously come down to the goal in mind and a weight training specific text will assist with building the right workout. Try to target the exercises as specifically as possible to a weakness you notice in your climbing. Extra weight training that is not really necessary is not only a waste of time that could be better spent, but it might add unnecessary muscle tissue and extra training load to recover from. Whole body exercises like clean and jerk, 'supermans' and 'spidermans' as well as bar work like front levers, one arm locks or pull-ups (often assisted) are all good for the body strength required in climbing moves. If bouldering and weights are to be done in the same day, it generally works best to do the bouldering first while you feel fresh and sharp, both for performance, training benefit and safety from injury.

The climbing starved

If you have a job that takes you away from home for intermittent or sustained periods or you live in a place very distant from any rock or local climbing wall, build your own, however small or temporary, or take a fingerboard with you before resorting to weights. If the weights really are the only option, they are far better than losing all your hard earned strength by doing nothing. Even just a little weights could be enough to maintain your strength levels while you wait it out for your next chance to climb. The variety of stimulus can be exactly what a lot of people need who have quite a stagnant monotonous routine of climbing (always the same boards, crags, holds etc). Travelling with a set of Metolious rock rings will solve your fingerboard problem if you can't install one at your climbing starved location. Rock rings are basically a pair of resin holds on cord that can be attached to a bar, rafter etc. You can also make your own with a couple of small squares of ply and finger friendly edges that are about 20mm deep, incut but with a rounded edge that won't hurt your skin too much.

A good routine for keeping general climbing strength would be a warm-up followed by 30 minutes on the rock rings doing a standard fingerboard routine. After that you could move onto some lat pull-downs or one arm pull-ups, seated rows, front levers and a handful of triceps dips. The rests between the sets could be used to do some hip stretches for flexibility. If you have more time left over after all this you could do some running or other cardiovascular work for general health or even recovery if the pace is gentle. Obviously you will need to tailor the exact content of the work to the available time and the priorities you have. For instance, a wiry and light climber who has a good finger strength to weight ratio but poor body strength for very powerful moves would make sure to include the full body exercises like front levers, but might only need a little fingerboard work to maintain strength until he goes back to real climbing. In contrast, the bulkier powerful (commonly male) climber who has a strong body and perhaps previous history of gym work might be better spending much of the time just on the deadhangs and one or two other body exercises that have been a little neglected of late.

If the spells away from climbing with access only to a weights gym are fairly short (like a week at a time with fairly big gaps), the variety effect could prove a really useful and productive way to break up a seasonal routine of climbing, target specific strength weaknesses and kickstart further improvement. Things get a little more complicated if the time out of climbing is nearly equal to the climbing time. It gets harder to avoid the negative effects of always training pure strength and not enough technique. Climbers should also be really careful to keep the workouts closely focused on the big strength priority for climbing, which is finger strength across the different grip types. There will be a particular challenge for climbers in this situation to gain climbing (forearm) endurance for their goal routes. So being organised to get as much volume of pumpy climbing when the opportunities arise will prevent endurance ending up as a critical weakness.

Some other situations

A little weight training can also be useful for some other special cases. It can often help to get beginner climbers over a critical basic threshold of body strength for moving on rock. Some female climbers who are very light can hang onto holds on entry level climbing wall routes, but really struggle to move between them due to very low upper body muscle mass. Things are okay on slabby routes, but even attempting vertical routes feels like too hard and off-putting. In most cases, access to some just off-vertical routes will be the most efficient way to gain a level of basic strength that will get you moving on steeper ground and open up more possibilities of routes to try at climbing walls and crags. However, it might be that a little supplementary work in the gym could speed the process up. Lat pull downs are the exercise to do if it's not possible to manage a pull-up on a bar.

At the other end of the scale, those at an advanced level could use weights to train for a very specific movement - perhaps an unusually powerful single movement on a route, or an usual feature like cracks or horizontal roofs. Use your imagination to imitate the movement required as closely as possible in the weights exercises. But always after considering the methods for doing the same job in a climbing situation. For instance, could you replicate the movement on a bouldering wall with bigger holds but using a weight belt and/or poorer footholds. If you have the time, a combination of both may well be most effective. An example of this in action would be training for a route with very powerful undercut moves. Some weights (seated rows and bicep curls) might help to replicate the dynamic part of the movements, and holding powerful static positions on undercuts on a steep board will prepare you for the locking strength required to reach off the undercuts.

Summary: Weights can be called into action to very effectively solve some specific problems that crop up due to circumstances, injury etc. Outside of these specific cases where there is a clear benefit from using them, they are a poor substitute for more specific exercises, especially real climbing. They have a place in training for climbing, but it's easy to overuse them at the expense of more effective training of the whole system by climbing.

To the wiry

We've seen earlier in the book that the skinny climber has a lot of advantages, a great starting place to develop good technique and physique for hard climbing. His number one worry is to settle into the comfort of the types of moves he will be naturally good at - fingery small moves. He will be the one most likely to be able to hang on for ages (his light body not getting pumped too fast) and try to find a small hidden hold to make the crux work for him. However, he's the one likely to hit a brick wall when there is no intermediate small hold, only a big or very powerful move.

If the wiry climber puts in the hours on the really burly problems, seeking out the most brutal of moves between positive holds, and spends time climbing with the beefcakes, some of this natural disadvantage can be offset. Perhaps even a little basic body strength work in supplement will speed up the process, helping them lock sidepulls to their hip, pull in on steep undercuts and move their feet around on distant footholds on the horizontal roofs. If they can do this, not for a few weeks and then forget about it, but week in, week out for years, then they will have the best of both worlds and overtake everyone else.

To the beefcake

The strength in the body is there, but will you be able to actually apply it to the rock? Maybe you got it from a previous life of sport or weight training, or just naturally. Either way, strength training is a satisfying and thus addictive pastime - you are always the best, in the gym anyway. But all that time in the gym or doing climbing wall routes footless for fun was time missed to actually learn how to climb. When you slap for the hold on the crux move, you visualise your hand crushing the next hold and grunt out loud. In the process, the feet are forgotten, heels are relaxed and lift off the footholds and you swing. Maybe you are even strong enough to absorb that too? But after 20 moves of spending strength like it's going out of fashion, it runs out before the end of the route. Meanwhile the skinny, talented climber struggled to get between the holds from the very first move. Their feet didn't come off once. They are still struggling at the last move, but they haven't fallen.

Seek out the moves that cannot be tamed by strength alone. Let them force you to really look at the rock, try to understand the subtle movement possibilities that could make the moves work and learn to really climb. Apply the strength you have to all your points of contact, and right through the move. Don't forget to pull with the feet as you reach and slap aggressively with the hand.

What muscle ballast do you have that you don't need? More real climbing and less time on the campus board or the gym might well make your strength personal bests take a hit. But what are you training for? The bottom line is that the best climber tends to be the one who is quite good at every performance aspect, not exceptionally strong and not trying to bully the rock into submission.

81

To the tall

Go faster; you are too heavy to sloth around on tiny holds! Not too fast so you can't look where your feet are going, but you need to train yourself to move with momentum and the 'snap' of the midget climbers. Your height will get you to the distant holds on a handful of moves, but the rest of the moves will be harder because the holds feel so small to support your big body. High peak forces during the reaching move because you are trying to be static will quickly exceed your reserves of finger strength. Start low, generate the momentum from those big powerful legs and get the next hold quickly. For good examples, spend some time climbing with short climbers who climb like circus acrobats. Notice how they have several inches less reach than you but can do the big moves you can't reach.

Being on the tall side and being overweight is doubly bad news for finger strength:weight ratio. Every percentage point of excess body fat lost has a bigger effect than for a shorter climber. So it's really worth it.

To the lucky little ones

Small holds feel big, not just because you can get more finger in them, but you are light enough to hang on too. It's getting between the holds that is the problem. Sure it's a disadvantage, if you are trying to reach statically and lock small holds to your chest or your hip. So move with momentum. Your light body can catch the holds at speed and hold on. Use all the tricks you can to make your reach bigger. Twist your trunk as you move to add the length of your shoulder girdle to your reaching arm. Use the momentum to throw your hips into the wall so at the point of catching the hold, your body is close to the wall and your weight is thrown over your feet which can stretch up as far as possible. Milk your small body and limbs as much as you can - reach deeper into holds with hands, or jam toes or heels in pockets. Get two hands on where bigger climbers could only fit one. Maybe you can climb inside the really big holds by throwing a whole leg or arm inside huge pockets? Or squeeze into tight bridging positions in tiny corners and grooves to rest?

Milk the natural advantages when performing, attack the weaknesses in training. Most don't. They are stuck trying to perform all the time, and never really training.

When you really can blame your tools

The rockboot pain cycle: Beginners buy roomy sized, symmetrical, floppy entry level rockboots > They feel that a higher spec performance shoe might help them climb, so they buy the ones they see good climbers wearing > They don't fit the feet correctly and make climbing for any length of time agonising > Not wanting to give up easily, especially having spent a lot of money, they persevere, until the agony makes them hate the shoes with a passion > They crack and go back to the old floppy pair.

Sometimes this cycle goes around several times in a climber's career and rockboots feel like the bane of the sport to them. It's unnecessary. Performance rockboots should hug the feet and have a snug fit. But above all, they should fit. Because the shoes have to hold their own shape to do their job of focusing the force from your feet onto a small area at the toe, the shoe has to fit your foot extremely well from the outset. Some shoes do have a little stretch and mould a little to the shape of your foot. Not all do however, and even then it will be a small amount. The key mistake when choosing a pair for yourself is simply not to try enough pairs on. The last shape used by certain models, or even by certain manufacturers must be a good fit for your foot. If not, keep looking. Source a shop that has a large range and try everything on, making a shortlist of a few that felt like a really nice snug but comfortable fit with no pressure points. Make sure you try walking and standing on edges in them to confirm they still feel good in these situations. Once you find a model that works well and feels good and comfortable to climb in, stick to it. If you see it's going on sale or out of production, stockpile a few pairs now to save you the bother of starting the search all over again.

If you do make a mistake and buy a pair you can't suffer, take it on the chin and save up for a new pair. Whatever you do, don't go back to the old, tired, floppy beginner boots. You won't just be losing the precision of high quality boots, you'll be setting yourself up for permanently bad footwork. Here's why:

All technique is a collection of habits of movement you have adopted. Certain external conditions set you up to adopt particular habits, which could be good or bad for your climbing. Whichever is the case, they are extremely hard to change once you have them, even if you change the external conditions.

83

The habits stick around. If you climb in entry level, baggy or tired rockboots and start to progress onto small footholds, think of what happens as you fight your way up hard climbs. You try to solve the crux moves by placing your feet well, but they keep skidding. You can't apply force through the floppy rubber and you can't get the big toe into the most incut part of the hold because of the big rounded toe box. As you wobble and struggle with the footholds, you run out of time and use brute upper body strength to attempt the move. Each time this happens, a subconscious message is stored in the movement planning part of the brain - "Don't use footwork as a first resort, it doesn't work as well as the arms for solving problems". This, of course, is the exact opposite of the learning you want to happen. Do this for a year, and that clocks up to many thousands of these reminders for the brain; an engrained habit of poor footwork is born and ready to live a long time in your technique. The situation is quite similar if you are wearing a performance shoe that doesn't fit well. Except the stimulus to the brain is the pain you get when you really try to apply force through ill-fitting shoes.

The earlier in your climbing career you move to a well fitting performance shoe, the less bad habit accumulation you will have to undo and the deeper and wider your footwork repertoire will become.

Sort it now.

Campus boards hurt almost everyone

Campus boarding is among the most dangerous methods of training for climbing. It's not as dangerous as climbing with poor technique, but nearly everyone who does campusing for sustained periods has problems with finger or elbow injuries sooner or later. To reduce this risk, first of all make sure the campus board is safe. Many climbing walls make awful campus boards that destroy the elbows of their users. The main problem is when they are not steep enough. Ideally a campus board should be steep enough that the elbows don't fully lock down on big moves and the knees don't knock the board on the second move of a 1-4-7 laddering sequence. The aggressive deep locks that happen when the board is not steep enough are perfect for developing elbow epicondylitis. Campus boards should be placed somewhere cool and dry and if possible out of the way of climbers who put their feet on the rungs. Foot polished campus rungs are slippery and excellent for tweaking finger pulleys. Take a little fine sandpaper to the rungs to take the shoe rubber and grime out of the wood and restore good friction.

Like fingerboarding and other basic strength exercises, campus boards really come into their own for really experienced and elite climbers who have a vast volume of real climbing under their belts and have superb technique with which to apply the extra strength gained. Youth climbers or those who only have a few short years background in climbing would get more benefit from good, powerful, varied bouldering. Once again the exceptions are where there simply isn't access to good bouldering regularly enough. Using a campus board might be a useful supplement if the bouldering at your local climbing centre is very limited, not steep enough and rarely changed. However, it will always be a second option, never a first resort.

Climbers have found various inventive ways to use the campus board, but simple laddering will be the most effective and safe method for most people. Because of the high forces and sudden loading, extreme care should be taken using a crimp grip on the campus board. There is rarely a sound case for doing this anyway as there is so much crimping in normal bouldering. Progressing from a simple 1-2-3 and matching hands on the finishing rung, to 1-3-4, 1-3-5 and so on will provide a good path of progression to bigger moves. Don't get hung up by trying to perform on the campus board. This is training, so get the right balance between intensity and volume. Climbers often spend all their time trying the next laddering level that is just out of reach and no time doing repeated sets on the level they can complete with difficulty. If you can nearly do 1-5-8, spend most of the time doing 1-4-7, maybe building up to reversing it as well, until you reach a level when you can regularly complete 1-5-8 instead of just trying it and failing all the time.

Above all, don't get addicted to it, or turn into the long-faced gorilla.

Climbing is not a cardiovascular sport

Misunderstanding the metabolic challenge of rock climbing is the root of many poor planning decisions in a climber's training. Let's get things clearer. Climbing rock is not really a cardiovascular fitness dependent sport. Leaving aside the primarily strength sport of bouldering for now, most rock routes present a local anaerobic endurance challenge. This is true both of routes that take less than a minute to complete and of routes that take over an hour to complete. 'Local' means the centre of fatigue is in the muscle (in this case the forearm) rather than a limitation of the whole cardiovascular system. 'Anaerobic' means that the oxygen supply cannot meet the metabolic demands of the muscle. It is by nature short lived, as the muscle cannot sustain the unfriendly chemical environment of anaerobic metabolism for long. In most sports, the chemical reaction pathways of anaerobic metabolism are used because metabolism is running too fast for the aerobic system to replenish energy for further contraction. This is true in hard climbing too, but the nature of static contractions of the forearm muscle when we grip holds also limits aerobic metabolism by squeezing muscle blood vessels shut under pressure, interrupting the supply of oxygen.

Route climbing is rarely a continuous, sustained metabolic war of attrition like distance running or cycling. The intensity is constantly rising and falling past the threshold for anaerobic metabolism to kick in. It comes in bursts of anaerobic effort with aerobic recovery. So both aerobic and anaerobic endurance are needed. But doesn't that further confuse matters? It's not just the type of metabolism we need to look at. The location is critical to understanding the metabolic picture.

Where is climbing endurance?

It's fairly obvious to climbers that the forearm is the centre of fatigue during most rock climbing. The reason for this is that the fingers have to operate at a high proportion of their maximum force for a large volume of time compared to other muscle groups. We understand that the fatigue is concentrated here because that's where the pain of muscle fatigue occurs. Contrary to common understanding, the byproduct of anaerobic metabolism in the hard worked forearm muscles, lactic acid, doesn't build up to spectacularly high levels in the bloodstream during climbing. Other sports like running that use bigger muscle groups and dynamic contraction reach much higher levels of blood lactate than climbing. The significant detail of forearm muscle activity in climbing is that the contractions are isometric. Isometric means the contraction is held statically (while the fingers grasp the hold) without the muscle changing length. During high force pulls on holds, little or no blood can flow in or out of the finger flexor muscles due to the high pressure squeezing the blood vessels shut. So chemicals cannot be removed or delivered to help metabolism keep going.

Unfortunately the picture of muscle fatigue isn't even as simple as that. Lots of chemical exchanges must happen at extremely fast rates to maintain sustained high force muscle contraction. The maximum speed of chemical pumps in muscle cells and the changes in concentrations of several different metabolic chemicals all contribute to reduced speed, coordination and force of contractions as we try to push the muscle to its limits.

Unlike other sports that feature continuous bouts of anaerobic effort, in climbing we do give our forearms very brief rest periods as we reach for the next hold. Occasionally, the rests are slightly longer if we reach a shake-out hold. During these, blood can move through the muscle to help remove acid and deliver oxygen once more. Yet climbing is unlike cardiovascular sports where moving muscles pump blood through themselves much more effectively and performance becomes limited by the rate the heart can move the blood between the lungs and muscles. Climbing endurance is not limited by the volume of blood pumped by the heart, even during rests. Quite apart from the anaerobic nature of high intensity climbing, the small muscles of the forearm cannot consume oxygen at a rate that would be limited by cardiovascular performance. It follows that general cardiovascular training to strengthen the heart has little influence on our ability to climb pumpy routes. In general, the adaptations that give us better forearm endurance for intermittent isometric contractions in climbing happen inside the forearm muscle.

What does limit forearm blood flow during rest periods is the density of tiny blood vessels (capillaries) in the muscle. Capillary density increases and decreases in a matter of weeks in response to rises and falls in the demand for high blood flow rates in a given muscle (not whole body). Aerobic enzymes and various other elements of the physical and chemical architecture of muscle cells also increase in concentration in response to aerobic activity of that muscle. The primary driver for capillary density adaptations is probably the repeated high pressure on the capillary walls, this occurs either in recovery from anaerobic (high intensity) bouts of climbing, or lighter aerobic bouts. The little research available into the intermittent contractions of the forearm in climbing suggests that a large part of climbing endurance comes down to the ability of the muscle to reach high levels of blood flow between contractions. Increases in the anaerobic capacity of the forearms comes from increases in various anaerobic enzymes.

To ensure maximum gains in climbing endurance, it is therefore vital that the endurance training mimics the real activity as closely as possible. General cardiovascular fitness may help us deal with the demands of a heavy training schedule, but won't contribute directly to forearm endurance and may actually interfere with more specific gains by adding another aspect of training stress for the body to recover from. Climbing endurance training means working the forearms, and the best way to do this is by real climbing. This climbing should have an anaerobic (short intense bouts) and aerobic (long, less intense routes) component. This holds even for those only wishing to do fairly short sport routes of less than one minute duration, because the increased capillary density gained through climbing longer routes will help to sustain hard moves by perfusing the muscle better during the brief moments between pulling on holds.

Endurance activities

The first question to deal with when choosing how to train endurance for climbing is the practicality of it. Clearly, the goal is to get high volumes of pumpy moves and routes completed on a regular basis. Often, there is a practical limitation of access to either the routes, or partners to belay and share the training with you. So, using a bouldering wall to do extended circuits carries some big advantages. This will be especially useful for very experienced climbers or those doing a high volume of real routes as well. They will have well developed tactics and the training will be purely about increasing fitness. For less experienced climbers, the learning of all the other skills of route climbing such as leading confidence, route reading and tactics are also essential objectives to fit into the training. For these climbers, the more of the climbing that can be done on real routes, the better, so long as they are steep and intense routes that develop good pacing and work the muscles hard enough.

The psychological effects of endurance training on your technique are not to be underestimated. Activities like low level traversing on a bouldering wall are likely to increase your fitness, but applied wrongly they can seriously mess up your climbing technique and negate any positive effects. It's not that the physical effect of the training is somehow drastically different in traversing, as is often misunderstood. The problem is that you get used to the type of movement and pattern of fatigue you get from the traversing, and when you go back to real routes, the difference feels unsettling and you don't climb well. Commonly, traverses are long, aerobic bouts of several minutes and you design them so you get a little pumped and stay at this level of fatigue throughout. While this is good for stimulating capillary growth, it's different from the normal routine of getting more and more pumped on a route, culminating in a fight just before the top. Also, the moves tend to be front on to the rock and quite small and so you get used to this type of move when you are pumped. When it comes to doing a long, aggressive move high on a route, it feels unnatural. All this is not to say that traversing shouldn't be done. But where it is used, it should be punctuated by regular sessions on real routes and shorter anaerobic routes or circuits.

Where you are using routes for training, it's nearly always a good idea to climb on lead, for the opportunity to work on your leading, falling and tactical skills and to get used to climbing on real leads when pumped. However, for more advanced climbers, who feel very confident with their leading skills, bouldering wall circuits are an extremely time efficient way to train endurance, especially anaerobic endurance.

The most effective arrangement of loading to train anaerobic endurance is interval training. Basically this just means successive short bouts with short rests in between, as opposed to one all out burst to complete failure. Failure point is still reached, but on the last set of the session. Ideally the fatigue should build steadily as each circuit is completed. Doing it this way means there is more activity done in the correct range of intensity over time than trying to fit it all into one bout. However, once you are already fairly fit, it is actually possible to perform an entire session in one bout by doing a hard circuit interspersed with a good aerobic rest at a shake-out, so you only step off the wall at the end of the last hard circuit (collapse in a heap might be more accurate).

The ideal length for an anaerobic bout is between 45-90 seconds. Whether you want to be in the lower or upper end of this range depends on the length of climbs you want to excel at. If you need both, then a mix of both lengths of circuit is best. Circuits of 25-50 hand movements tends to be about right because you climb slightly faster on circuits you know well than on real routes. This is also about the length of most climbing wall routes, so they are ideal for anaerobic training. Having said this, climbing wall routes are often not as sustained as they could be. Routes often have an easier start and finish, or are more cruxy in nature, interspersed with good rests. So there is a trade off between gaining leading skills and fitness by anaerobic training on routes, and better fitness gains from setting really sustained and personally tailored boulder circuits. The more experienced and confident you are, the more the decision leans towards using the bouldering wall for convenience. But some climbing walls have a good steep leading wall and a poor bouldering wall that isn't steep enough for endurance circuits. The decision is a personal one.

Setting anaerobic boulder circuits

The goal is for the circuit to be very sustained and develop a steadily increasing pump. So any particularly hard moves or even just very 'sketchy' moves that are easy to slip off will tend to upset the training effect. Choose a steep wall; 30-45 degrees is ideal. Make the moves relatively simple and basic and if possible on positive holds, but as fingery as your climbing level allows. Setting is a real skill that takes a fair bit of trial and error to perfect. You can work around this if you are inexperienced by copying another climber's circuit if you train at a climbing wall. Adapt it you suit your level by adding or removing holds or moves. The key mistake is to get hung up on sticking to the circuit once you have done the initial set. View your circuit as a 'draft' and don't be scared to change it if it's too hard or easy or you keep slipping off on an overly difficult move. Again, don't let performing get in the way of training. The ideal intensity will cause you to complete it (after familiarising yourself with the moves) with a significant pump on the first set. Rest for 2-5 minutes between sets and try to complete 4-7 sets of the circuit. Ideally on the last set you should be fighting and battling just to complete the circuit.

The aerobic component

Although anaerobic circuits do primarily train the anaerobic capacity of the forearms, there is likely to be a local aerobic training effect as well. The contractions while pulling on holds will be fully anaerobic because the blood supply is occluded and such high energy demand can only be met by anaerobic metabolism. However, the muscle will be very highly perfused during gaps in contractions while you reach between holds and between the circuits. This should stimulate aerobic adaptations too, especially capillary growth. Once you are reasonably fit on a circuit, you can increase the aerobic training effect of the anaerobic circuit by resting at a shake-out on the rock instead of stepping off the wall. This method effectively combines both types of training to create a very time efficient, but demanding session. Readers who are into running will have heard of the analog in that sport, known as 'Fartlek' training which uses intermittent sprints and slower aerobic recovery runs back to back.

If you feel it would be better to stick to routes for all your endurance training, either because you need the leading skills training or because of the lack of a good bouldering wall to use, you have two choices. You could either do anaerobic and aerobic routes separately, or combine them by climbing up a hard (anaerobic) route and back down a much easier (aerobic) route.

If doing them separately, then climbing up, back down and back up a route that's steep but well below your limit will work well. You can do this in the same session as the anaerobic circuits if your fitness level is up to it, doing the aerobic routes last in the session.

Understanding fatigue symptoms

Feedback from your forearms and how your climbing level changes during the session will help inform you if you are getting the correct intensity for training endurance. If you are doing anaerobic circuits/routes correctly, the first circuit should produce a reasonably significant pump in the forearm and deep and fast breathing should be immediately noticeable. By the third or fourth circuit you should be feeling a very deep and quite painful forearm pump with the muscle feeling firm to the touch and gasping for breath at the end of the circuit. By the final circuit you should be fighting with 100% effort just to complete the circuit, elbows winging out, gasping for breath, wide eyed and with sometimes nauseatingly painful pump in the forearm. After you get to this stage, you can stop and resume the next session the following day. Attempting to continue will completely exhaust the muscle fuel store which takes a lot longer to recover from and will end up reducing the overall training volume.

91

Aerobic circuits on routes should produce a deeper forearm pump, different in character to anaerobic high intensity bouts. The pump is still painful to a degree, but without the sharp acid burn of anaerobic bouts. Unless you have just started the training phase and are still quite unfit, the forearm is unlikely to be hard to the touch either. Instead it will feel hot and flushed with blood, but as the circuit goes on, strength will drain as the pump gradually overtakes the muscle. Breathing will never be in deep gasps recruiting the ribs for inhalation, but it will be elevated and steady.

In contrast to either of these, exhaustion of the muscle's 'fuel tank' of glycogen at the end of a long session of climbing is not really being pumped, but is often mistaken for it. This happens either after many hours straight climbing, or too many consecutive days training for the body to recover from, or if you've not eaten enough carbohydrate at the right time to replenish the glycogen store. This feeling is one of rapid and extreme loss of strength, such that even the strongest climbers can no longer hold onto massive holds. The loss of strength isn't really accompanied by painful pump, although the muscles are likely to be complaining generally about being exhausted, and if you rest for several minutes, your strength does not substantially recover. If you get to this stage during a session, stop, go home and eat a pile of carbohydrate rich food. Continuing serves no useful purpose either for learning technique or gaining fitness. In fact, exhausting the last 15% of the glycogen store could add a day or more onto your recovery time, and so will drastically reduce the total training volume you can complete over the longer term.

Endurance rules

With strength training, it's important to be relatively fresh to be able to generate the necessary forces to train strength properly. Training endurance is different. It's desirable to work yourself pretty hard and feel pretty tired. Even if you can still feel the last session in your arms by the start of the next, that's okay. In fact that's where you want to be. Once you warm up again, the muscles should stop complaining and work fine. If they don't and your level is well below the previous session and dropping fast, it's better to stop - you've exhausted the tank. You'll get a sense with experience of what to expect of your body, but never stop experimenting, because your capacity to absorb training is a constantly moving target that is dependent on a huge variety of disparate components.

In general, quite a few sessions per week is required to make gains in climbing endurance. Many climbers will make continued gains on three sessions a week, and as little as one session a week should maintain a given level during busy periods or if you've overdone it. More advanced climbers will be able to have far more sessions than this. Short, intense sessions of circuits 6 days a week is perfectly achievable if you have a big foundation of fitness and your body is well used to training over years. Elite level climbers might have 2 sessions a day for periods of the year! As always, let your body's response be your guide.

Unlike strength training, endurance will respond very much quicker, and significant gains can be made in just a few weeks. If you start from scratch, after some time off or just bouldering, the first week will be painful and hard work. The second week will show some improvements but still feel uphill. Often in the third week you'll really feel 'in the groove' and able to tolerate the training much better, as well as feeling significantly fitter. After five or six weeks of optimal training, the results will start to tail off. Of course, further gains are there for those who keep pushing the body, but often a change of focus back to strength will keep things fresh.

Often you'll want to combine a few different aspects of training in the same visit to a crag or climbing wall. The rule here is fairly simple: the highest force requiring aspects should always be performed earliest in the session. So in a theoretical training session where you did one of everything, the progression through the session wold go like this:

Warm-up > Basic strength > hard bouldering > easier bouldering > Anaerobic circuits/routes > Aerobic circuits/routes.

Part 3
Fear of falling: the real problem, probably…

The big four - movement technique, finger strength, endurance and body mass form a huge part of what helps you get through the hard moves and to the top of routes. Climbers these days are much better than they were at training at least a few of these components. So why has the general, average grade level of the climbing population not risen much more in the past fifteen years, with climbing centres in nearly every city?

What if there was a problem that interrupts the flow of benefit from improving the big four into our climbing performance? A separate component that puts a lid on the effect of any other effort we make to improve our climbing? That problem does exist and it affects a massive amount of climbers. It's not possible to put any firm numbers on the scale of it, but I've observed it as the primary weakness in over 50% of climbers I meet for coaching sessions.

That problem is fear of falling. It is the most insidious and unpleasant to deal with of perhaps any of the challenges that hard climbing presents. In part it is borne out of a very healthy instinct for self preservation and avoidance of pain. Humans are not hard wired to deal with fear of falling in an objective way. Our minds aren't set up to naturally assess the true risks of climbing and falling off. In most climbing situations that occur - sport climbing indoors or out, and bouldering and some trad climbing, falling off is, comparatively speaking, exceptionally safe. Yet for more than half of us it's a terrifying thought.

The drive to the climbing wall is more dangerous than taking a normal leader fall on one of the routes. However, the greater danger of the drive probably didn't even register in our thoughts, yet when we are above the protection bolt, losing strength or unable to figure out the next move, the prospect of falling a few metres onto the rope consumes our entire focus with crippling fear.

It's not this bad for everyone; fear of falling is a continuum from avoiding leading at all costs and climbing feeling like a constant battle, to reckless fearlessness at the other end. For some climbers, it's only a significant limitation to performance in certain situations, such as when very close to their limit, or on certain types of route such as overhanging terrain. In some ways this can be the worst situation, because those climbers rarely realise by themselves that they have a real problem with fear of falling. They simply justify their own choices and route preferences, and if climbing partners actually notice this, they are rarely direct enough to suggest that fear of falling is the real force that decides which climbs you try.

By the time climbers notice in themselves that fear of falling is starting to dictate the types of climbs they are willing to attempt, it's usually a very significant weakness. What usually happens is the climber considers forcing themselves to move above protection and out of their comfort zone, but the prospect of this seems too unpleasant to actually do. So instead they settle for working within that comfort zone and reason that it doesn't affect their climbing so long as they only try routes that don't feel scary. Unfortunately it's not true. Once again, the components of performance in climbing do not act independently, but affect each other directly. Fear of falling if left unchecked, changes your movement technique in a subtle way, making it more inefficient and affecting you on every climb you try.

In part one we saw the need for use of momentum in climbing in order to move efficiently. When climbers are trying to avoid even safe falls, they try to 'over control' climbing, making the moves as static as they can. On the hardest moves, they tend to over grip the holds as well, in case some aspect of the move becomes out of control, such as a foot slipping. This introduces huge inefficiency not only by losing the energy saving effect of momentum use, and pulling harder than is needed on the holds, but it also slows everything down. It's a negative feedback loop. The more inefficient the climbing becomes, the more you get pumped on routes and feel like you'll fall, and this feels scary.

The technique sabotage process:

Fear of falling > try to move statically > climbing becomes inefficient > climbing feels harder > more fear > slower and even more static movement

There is only one way to break this cycle, and everyone can do it, even the worst cases.

The only way

Above I said that fear of falling is the most unpleasant of all climbing's challenges to deal with. That's true when it comes to initiating an attack on it. However, it's also one of the most responsive and simple aspects to train, so long as the training is applied in the correct way. Unlike many other aspects of training for climbing, the hardest training session in 'falling confidence' is the first one, and if more training is carefully applied, each session will be easier than the last.

The problem is so common because we are hard wired to feel that falling is wrong. Our evolutionary training has passed onto us a sense that falling off above a drop means certain death, so it's no wonder it has such huge effect. Our minds aren't geared up to factor in and accurately measure the safety of our protection systems in climbing. We can read data that informs our rational brain that driving to the climbing wall carries a much higher risk of serious injury than falling off a bolted route with a competent belayer holding the rope, but in the moment of the climb and about to fall, our primal gut instinct overrides this. Our head can readily accept that falling is safe, but to our gut, it is unnatural. Thankfully, it can be retrained.

The only way to retrain our gut instincts to accept something that feels wrong is to show it, time after time. This means practice falls. Most climbers reading this book will probably have read this before and some will actually have tried it. They will have gone to a safe sport climb, with a good belayer and taken some deliberate falls in an effort to just get used to them. A month down the line, they are no further forward. Why?

It wasn't enough!

Earlier I compared the danger of falling off in climbing to driving. Consider the very first time you got behind the wheel of a car and pulled away on an urban street, or the first time you drove on a busy motorway. It was nerve-racking because the only way you could measure the danger was by using your gut instincts. You are steering through fast moving obstacles from second to second with little time to react and aware that an error could have serious costs. It's extremely stressful! Then, after just a handful of hours, the feeling has virtually disappeared and what once had your heart racing barely even registers in the conscious brain. It was nerve-racking at first because of unfamiliarity. There is nothing for our pre-programmed gut instincts to compare this experience to and measure the risk. There is no short cut to the pain of retraining it for those horrible first few hours. The striking thing about this comparison is that if you have spent any decent amount of time driving on fast roads, chances are you have seen first hand evidence of the risk, passing life changing or destroying accident scenes. And yet they have remarkably little effect on the way we drive. Our familiarity with our own seemingly safe world of our own car insulates us from the quite significant danger we are under. This phenomenon demonstrates ably the power of mental conditioning.

The opposite is true in climbing. Above a bolt, even a long way, the odds are we are exceptionally safe, and falling will give us nothing more than a momentary buzz. Our gut telling us falling off cliffs is wrong, together with unfamiliarity, is enough to make us feel exactly the opposite. The only way to correct this is to clock up falls - and not just one or two; hundreds.

Even though most climbers do make an effort to step out of their comfort zone, go for it a tiny bit more and take some small practice falls, their mistake is not to do enough. Not even nearly enough. Most people will practice falls for one session - maybe taking two or three falls - and then forget about it. The effect from even this tiny training input is noticeable, but it doesn't last. The main message of this section of the book is to practice falls day in, day out for months and years. Measure your practice falls in hundreds. How many exactly depends entirely on how bad the fear of falling is and how long the habit of avoiding falls has been engrained. Using myself as an example, 5-10 leader falls per session for a year was enough to break the irrational fear. Another couple of years of this was enough that the thought of falling no longer altered my technique in a negative way during my climbing. A further decade of this sort of volume of falls, built into my daily climbing was enough to stress-proof my confidence to allow me to make good, clear decisions about moves while right on the limit of falling, in situations when the fall was potentially unsafe.

Taking this history, we are talking about many thousands of leader falls to go from fear consuming most of my focus while leading, to feeling very confident and consistent on climbs that are demanding of leading confidence.

Of course only a small proportion of these were really big falls. I'm guessing that 70% of them were with the protection point near my feet or even less. I've maybe only taken less than 100 falls over 12 metres, and less than 15 over 20 metres. These big falls happened when I was ready for them and so they made big deposits in the bank account of leading confidence. Despite all this practice, the skill is still reversible like any other aspect of preparation for climbing. If no falls are taken for a few months, it takes several weeks of practice to regain the previous highpoint of confidence.

Another point is that not all of these many falls contribute positively to your confidence. The familiarity you need is not simply familiarity with falling per se, it's familiarity with falls that went okay. A single bad experience with falling can instantly wipe out months or even years of confidence gains. So the technique with which the falls and the practice is applied is critical so you don't make things worse.

Falling technique

There are three main elements that determine whether a fall will feel fine and add to confidence, or go badly and knock a huge chunk off it. These are the preparation for the fall, the fall itself, and the swing in (note: I'm talking about straightforward falls on sport routes for now).

Anything that reduces unknown quantities in your mind when preparing for a fall will have a huge effect on your composure when you feel you are about to come off. First, make a mental note as you clip each piece of protection that you have clipped it properly and it looks okay, so you don't start to doubt it once you're wobbling above it. When you feel like you are likely to fall, one of the biggest worries is that your belayer is aware of what's going on and is ready to catch you. Let them know! The most common way is to shout "watch me". Note: if you over use it, it becomes pointless. I've seen climbers say "watch me" over a hundred times during a pitch in a near continuous chant reminiscent of watching Kabadi. How is the belayer meant to know when you are really about to fall? It helps both of you if you explain your situation a bit more, especially if you are a long way up the pitch and they can't easily see you. "I'm going to have to jump for this hold, but I don't know it's a hold; watch me here" or, "I'm pumped. Nearly at the next clip; be ready to give me slack in a second." The latter message tells them you are looking at a bigger fall and to be careful with how much slack they let out and to be extra attentive for the next few moves. For you, it's simply one less thing to worry about.

If you realise you are not going to progress any further on the route but have time to prepare for the fall, look at the drop zone: where is the safest space to fall into? Is there a slab you might come close to, or are you going to take a big sideways swing? Prepare to push yourself in the best direction to make the fall as clean as possible and into the safest space. Let your belayer know again at the moment you start to fall. "Take!" or "I'm off!" are the most common shouts. Make sure the belayer knows in advance what that means and stick to it so there is no confusion (which will linger in your mind next time round).

As you start to fall, as hard as it may be, try not to slap pointlessly upwards or keep trying to hold on and slither down the rock. Initiate the fall as clearly and decisively as your confidence allows so you have a chance to exert some control over your trajectory. One of the big aspects that you can get wrong with initiating the fall is how far out from the rock to fall. If you try to hang on and slither into your fall, you risk hitting the rock surface as you fall straight down, and get tangled up in the rope or protection or get flipped uncontrollably during the fall. If you push out too far, you will clear any obstacles on the way down, but the swing in and resultant smash can easily be violent enough to cause injury and is much harder to control. On overhanging rock, falling straight down is fine, and even on off-vertical terrain only a very gentle push out from the rock is required to strike the correct balance between these two extremes. This aspect of falling technique is critical to get right. What's worse is that violent swings into the rock can actually be even harder during shorter falls or when the belayer takes the rope in tight before you fall. This often happens when climbers start to practice with small falls. They tell the belayer to take in more rope to make the fall feel less scary. However, the effect of the tight rope is that you whip around in an arc as you swing in. None of your momentum is lost and you hit the wall hard, often without enough time to brace hands and feet.

This bad technique sets up a negative feedback loop that makes it absolutely hopeless for making any progress with fear of falling. In fact things usually get worse. Determined to see some results you keep trying more falls.

Each one feels scarier than the last because the nasty slams are fresh in the memory. So you shout to the belayer to take tighter when you are about to let go to try and make this one less terrifying.

Good belaying during falls is obviously essential to avoid this downward spiral. The belayer should maintain a small amount of slack in the system wherever it's safe to do so. Falling off just below the second bolt of a route is an obvious exception - any extra slack here might risk a ground-fall. When the leader falls, the belayer, if not fixed to a belay, should move forward as the rope comes tight to absorb the shock more softly and prevent such a sharp swing in. The social dynamic between the leader and belayer is crucial here. Often a leader who is on a route that is out of their comfort zone or about to take some practice falls will put pressure on their belayer to take the rope tight before the leader lets go. It takes some courage and good social skills to negotiate with the leader before they start up the route to discuss, agree and reassure them that a little slack and a soft catch will make things much better. They won't always follow through when it comes to the moment of truth and demand a tight rope as they are about to drop. Ignoring them and giving slack anyway might seem like a good idea to 'teach' them that this makes a much nicer fall. But often undermining their instructions and breaking their sense of trust in you as the belayer will end up being counterproductive and cancelling out any benefits.

So the amount the leader pushes outwards when initiating the fall, and the belaying technique during it determines the speed of the swing into the wall. But this is not all that is important. The leader's technique for absorbing the impact with the wall, however gentle, is the final and crucial step in creating a positive falling experience. As early as possible during the fall, the climber should adopt a brace position ready to absorb any shock that occurs on the final swing in. The correct position is to lean back slightly and spread the arms and legs out in front of you ready to hit the wall. However, arms and legs should be slightly bent and not rigid. As you swing in and make contact with the wall, your feet should hit the wall first and should be able to absorb all the force. Even on an off-vertical wall, a fall (large or small) should only cause a mild swing in if the falling and belaying technique has been correct. The hands should rarely have to absorb any force and really just help to balance you and keep you upright. Nevertheless, getting into the habit of bracing them anyway is important for those times when the swing in ends up being a little worse for whatever reason. Ultimately they might protect your head from coming close to the wall in a really bad fall.

Once all of these steps are in place, falling in the vast majority of sport climbing and even well-protected trad climbing cases will be consistently trouble free. If you spend time looking around at a popular sport climbing destination or even a busy climbing wall, you'll see this in action, non-stop. Falling well is okay. Sadly, even if one of the above techniques is missing from the chain, the falling experience is bound to feel quite the opposite - a scary and even painful experience that's unlikely to leave you keen to try it more. Once you have all the elements and have your first leader fall that went well, you can start making small deposits of confidence, one at a time. However, getting lazy or resorting back to bad habits and ending up with a nasty falling experience will make a much bigger dent in your confidence than a single positive fall can repair. So discipline really pays of in the field of mental training. The only thing left to do once you are on the right track is get as far down it as possible and clock up those falls.

Practice indoors

You can start practicing falls anywhere it's safe to do so. Indoors is definitely the gentlest place to begin. The wall shapes are well suited to less hazardous drop zones and cleaner falls. Those starting from scratch with leading confidence should start off really easy. Skipping the first couple of hurdles by going straight in with substantial falls might end up with negative progress. The idea is to introduce one element at a time, and stay at that level until it's really easy before moving on. Start by letting go with the protection just below waist level or even on a slack top rope; just really enough to slump directly onto the rope. You can barely even call it a fall, but it's still the first hurdle. It convinces the mind that parting company with the rock is normal.

Next, fall with the gear at knee level. The length of the fall might be less than two metres (with rope stretch), but even at this length it's important for the belayer not to pull the rope tight before the fall in order to avoid a harsh slam into the rock. It's amazing how much momentum the body builds up in a split second of falling, and with such a short fall you'll not have time or room to brace your feet properly. Slamming knees and wrists off the wall or protruding holds is enough to cause injury even from a one metre fall.

102

The next stage is the fall with the protection at your feet. This is a really big change from the previous level. The increased rope paid out plus its stretch and the movement from the belayer to absorb your momentum will mean you go quite a lot further than you might expect. It feels like a 'proper' fall and it's this size of fall where you really get to practice and perfect all the techniques of falling. So it's important to take many falls (10-100 depending on how fast you progress) before moving onto bigger or more complicated falls. This level is the foundation to move onto bigger falls without them being too scary and having a counterproductive effect. The stronger this foundation, the better.

Only once you are comfortable with taking falls with the protection at or just below your feet without it even registering as a worry should you take on bigger practice falls, or falls in more intimidating situations on climbs. The next stage is obviously to take longer falls, building on the foundation to allow you to be more confident and able to stay focused on the climbing rather than worrying about falling when you get high above protection. Once you are at this level, the process isn't over. It's necessary to start to make your hard won confidence more resilient to the knocks it might take from novel situations or nasty surprises that routes might throw up. In sports psychology this is called 'stress proofing'. Basically the idea is to use your psychological (confidence) skills and falling (practical) skills in an ever widening net of potential situations. The effect is that when the time comes to call on your confidence and falling skills in a worst case scenario, the pressure of the new circumstances doesn't cause such a crisis that you fail to access and use the skills at all.

To continue your indoor falling skills practice, introduce new practice situations by using different belayers, on as many different wall angles as possible, when you've pulled up slack to clip the next bolt and in more pressured situations like a route you've been 'saving' for an onsight or a leading competition. The more diverse the situations you practice in, the more resistant your confidence will be to unusual scenarios and simply climbing at your limit. Notice I said 'continue', and not 'complete' your falling skills practice. Falling practice is never complete, because like any aspect of climbing preparation, it's reversible and if you don't use the skill regularly, it'll slide backwards at an alarming rate.

Practice on sport climbs

Unless you started out climbing outside on sport routes, moving onto falling practice outdoors will feel harder for most climbers. One of the biggest differences is with onsight climbing: you cannot always see the next bolt, you just have to climb until you do see it. This seemingly small difference from indoor climbing presents a massive challenge for those who struggle with fear of falling. The simple act of moving away from the last protection with no fixed target to aim for, relying only on trust in your own ability and that the solution will emerge as you move up can be incredibly hard to master.

This can be especially demoralising if you've already put a fair bit of time and effort into practicing your leading and falling indoors and on more straightforward sport climbs. There are no shortcuts to this next level. You simply have to start again with progressive exposure to the situations that you are struggling with and eventually gain a massive reservoir of familiarity. Pick a route where you know you'll not be able to see the next bolt or the route finding between bolts will be unobvious. Climb as high as you can bear above the bolt and take a controlled fall. Next time up, don't aim to complete the runout, just go one or two moves higher and take the fall again. Repeat until the fall feels so familiar it's almost boring to take it again. Some readers will be thinking, "But that could take all day!" Exactly.

Again, the key mistake in moving up the ladder of leading confidence is to underestimate the volume of practice needed at each stage to be ready to move to the next. Very few (the naturally daring) climbers haven't had to go through this process. However, many of them will have done it earlier in their climbing career when they were learning everything for the first time. So they didn't grudge it so much. The problem with those who have a long engrained fear of falling is that they subconsciously see themselves as relative experts in climbing. They have 'done their time' of learning from the ground up, so they don't want to have to go through the grind of extended practice of basic exercises over and over.

In actual fact, for the engrained habits it needs even more practice than would have been necessary if falling familiarity was gained from the outset. Engrained bad habits always take much longer to undo than creating good ones from a clean slate. There is no way round it. Once you can swallow that and accept that repetitive work needs done, you can start and the taste of real progress after the dull ache of plateau will revive the motivation.

Building falls into your daily climbing diet

Reading this, I imagine climbers might baulk at the thought of interrupting their 'real' climbing with such a large volume of practice falls. It's true that falling practice might need to be done in isolation as a separate exercise in the early weeks and months to bootstrap up the steep lower reaches of the improvement curve. However, it shouldn't take too long during a climbing session. Later, the falls should be built more and more into the normal climbing. The final stage of the process is when the falling practice and falls that happen as part of your normal climbing fully converge and you maintain the habit of regular falls and demanding leads as part of your standard climbing diet. At this point, it doesn't really feel like training any more, but obviously the result is the same.

At first, you can build falling practice into your climbing sessions by taking deliberate falls from just before the lower-off on indoor sport routes. To start with, you could fall from just above the last bolt, or complete the route without clipping the lower-off and downclimb a few moves to a good point to drop off. Later, drop from the finishing hold of the route without clipping the lower-off and eventually while pulling up some extra slack to make the fall a little larger again. If you do 20 routes in a session, 3 times a week, and practice fall from every one (why not?), that's a few thousand falls in a single year, for no extra time commitment whatsoever. Complete this simple task and it would be nearly impossible not to make huge gains in leading confidence, providing your falling technique makes these falls a positive falling experience. Poor falling technique will have the exact opposite effect, except it would only take a few tens of falls with an overly tight belay or without bracing the hands and feet well to cripple your confidence, if not your body.

In addition to this deliberate practice, you should clock up falls during your attempts on hard climbs you don't succeed on. Indoor walls are not helpful in this respect because of the easy escape routes that are just too tempting to use if you are scared to commit to a hard move and then fall. It's far easier to grab a different coloured hold or a quickdraw. Or since the bolts are so close together you can just shout "take" and sit on the rope. Most climbers who do this think that their confidence is staying static meantime. They know they are putting off trying to improve their boldness, but they think that so long as they keep doing what they do now they are not going backwards. Wrong.

We come back to the founding law of training: specificity. What you do you become. The habits you engrain become more and more calcified as time goes on. The more times you tell the brain that it's normal for a brightly coloured jug or a quickdraw to be available to grab any time the clock starts ticking on a hard route, the more it will melt in panic any time it's not there. The more you use it, the more you will need to lean on the crutch of being able to grab something instead of committing and potentially falling. So when you do eventually decide to tackle the problem, your experience will count against you. So start now.

Like breaking any addiction, different people will respond slightly differently depending on the strategy used to break the habit. Severe cases will need to take each easy route as it comes, refusing to grab a different colour on nearly every move. This takes a lot of determination, but it's the only way out of that particular pit for some. If the tendency to bail out only happens occasionally, like on hard routes or when you are really pumped, a more stringent approach sometimes works faster. Simply decide to go cold turkey and never, ever say "take" or grab any 'bail-out' hold or quickdraw except where there is clear danger involved. To succeed, it's much better if you tell your regular climbing partner of your commitment to make it more real and so they can encourage you at moments of determination or weakness. Like the deliberate practice falls, the earliest stages of this habit breaking are the hardest. With every week you wean yourself off shouting "take" and fighting on until the fall instead, the easier and more enjoyable it gets. It's really a matter of getting over the first couple of hurdles.

Outdoors, there aren't so many opportunities to avoid falls if you are leading hard routes. In this field, the clipstick is the enemy. If you find yourself relying on it in the slightest, give it away. If you take it to the crag, it will always be too tempting not to use it. It will beat you back to square one every time you try to break free from it.

Once you've put in the hours, disciplining yourself to make 5-20 falls occur per sport climbing day for, let's say, a year, the problem will be much smaller without doubt you'll be climbing 2-5 grades harder if it was a noticeable problem before. Once you get to this stage, the task is to make sure that regular falls becomes part of your normal climbing routine, so that you keep progressing and avoid losing the gains you made already. You'll no longer need to take deliberate falls, although if a particular route is unusually 'spooky' but you know it's safe, even the boldest climbers will practice a fall a few times just to fully eliminate it from their minds. You'll be taking regular falls by committing yourself fully on all your hard onsights and while working and attempting redpoints. If you're not falling off some of them, you should try some harder ones. You'll also be taking regular falls indoors on training routes that are close to your limit and boulder problems you are working. Try your best not to get complacent once you have become a confident leader and faller. Keep a rough mental note of the number of falls you are taking from month to month, and if it's been a while since you had the opportunity for some reason, make an extra effort to catch up with extra practice. A good example of this are experienced and relatively confident climbers who mainly train on bouldering walls due to their convenience. When they go on a sport climbing trip, the absence of regular falling exposure takes even the most hardened leader a bit of getting used to again. A first day of some decent practice falls will save a week of tentative and tight movement on the rock while you readjust.

Practice on trad

If you are a trad climber, then practice falls on sport climbs are an invaluable foundation to get used to the idea of falling per se. It is one less unknown quantity. Obviously, the variable nature of trad protection adds another layer of familiarity to be gained. While sport climbing falls are a foundation of trad leading confidence, they are no substitute. The real gains are made with falls onto real trad gear. As with getting used to falls in general, the technique to be applied is progressive exposure to falls further and further outside your initial comfort zone. If you avoid trad falls until the day when you take a substantial and unplanned fall, the result could be a huge dent in your confidence that some climbers wouldn't recover from. Starting early is key.

It's definitely best if you've got used to falling and learned the technique on sport routes first, so when you come to learn it on trad, the fact that it's natural protection is the only unfamiliar aspect being trained. Just like the sport climbing process, start easy with small falls onto solid and backed up gear. If you are not confident in your ability to place and be certain of the holding power of your gear placements, then take some formal training in climbing safety systems. Make sure you resist any temptation to grab the protection if you are falling from just above it. Not only does it mess up your falling technique and risk an uncontrolled swing into the wall, but you might pull your gear out! As you progress to bigger falls, keep using well protected routes where the gear is beyond doubt and backed up. Doubt in your mind about whether the gear will hold you risks the fall having a negative effect on your confidence rather than positive.

Progressing beyond this to a really high level of confidence with trad leading and falling is an incredibly subtle game of treading the line between pushing the boundary of your comfort zone outwards, little by little, and going too far and knocking a chunk out of it. Unplanned falls on hard trad onsights or redpoints, when they go well, can make large gains in confidence. However, they come with obvious danger when the protection is not perfect and one bad fall will make for long lasting psychological effects, not to mention any physical ones. Trad climbers venturing into this level will no doubt experience both types of fall, sooner or later. Actually, having some gentle 'frightener' falls where maybe the top piece of gear was not beyond doubt (that it will hold a fall) or there wasn't too much room to drop into above the ground can be good for your confidence in the long run. If you are confident and used to taking falls and going for it with your climbing, it's possible to get too confident, and pay for it with a really unpleasant fall that is very hard to recover from. Some gentle reminders that a balance between confidence and healthy, controllable fear really help to underpin your confidence. Once again, this area is a dangerous game of balancing confidence gains with the danger of taking falls that will dent confidence or cause injury. Be careful and err on the conservative side. Getting it wrong has high consequences.

When you just can't fall off

So far we've talked mostly about situations where falling is, objectively speaking, safe and the problem is with our interpretation of the danger and familiarity with the situations of falling. What about the trad protected climbs where falling off really is dangerous? When it's plain that there is not enough protection to prevent injury or worse if you fall. The best trad climbers have clearly found a way to manage fear in this high stakes game of mental and physical control. How do they manage it?

At this level, familiarity with falling generally, and trust in trad gear earned by falling onto good placements are pre-requisites. It is possible to perform well on hard bold trad routes without these, but very few climbers will manage it through inherent boldness they've gained from other experiences. Even those climbers could go further still if they practiced falling skills. In contrast, almost any climber can learn to feel safe within controlled limits if they are aware of and apply all the support systems and processes available. A comparison with other fields is useful again here. Bold climbing, like many other activities, can be transformed from an extremely risky activity to an acceptably safe one by rigorous application of safety systems. Without these, driving cars, flying aeroplanes, taking powerful medicinal drugs, having major surgery or deep sea diving would all be laughably risky. In these activities things do go wrong and there are severe consequences, almost always caused by failing to follow the safety systems that protect against the accidents. Bold trad is just like this.

The goal of the bold trad climber is to be able to have the correct mental conditions at all times to keep making good, clear decisions about what to do next. Once those decisions are made, it's about having the focus to act them out without hesitation or distraction. In other words, the trad climber needs to take steps to reduce the mental 'load' at any one time so that confusion and panic don't result in bad decisions.

The first stage in this process is eliminating unknowns. Unknown quantities make the mind imagine every possible outcome. There are lots of possible unknown quantities in climbing, so if you have to deal with too many during the climb, there isn't much mental space left over to concentrate on the decisions and the actual climbing. There are a plethora of possible outcomes, and not enough information to see how small the risk of the worst case scenarios are. The temptation to panic is overwhelming. Even in onsight climbing there are many unknowns which can be reduced or eliminated by thinking in advance. So the climbing challenge does not start at the first move of the route. In fact this is the last stage of the process of a good climbing performance. The more of these unknowns you can deal with in advance, the better you'll be able to deal with the ones that emerge during the climbing. Here are some of them:

- What falling feels like.
- What falling onto trad gear feels like.
- How long you can keep climbing when pumped.
- What the next gear placement is most likely to be.
- Where the next rest is.
- Whether you could be rescued from your current position.
- How far you will fall if you come off now.
- What is likely to happen during the fall.

If you have to process all of this on top of the actual climbing during the route, it gets too much and the quality of the assessments and decisions starts to fall apart. Some of the above questions can be eliminated by prior experience and practice. Being used to climbing at your limit, getting pumped and falling off during sport climbs or well protected trad climbs gives you experience of how your mind and body responds to these aspects, so you don't have to consider them consciously during a dangerous trad climb. They are still assessed and considered from moment to moment, but this can happen subconsciously. The rest of the unknowns can be either eliminated, or drastically reduced by viewing the route from the ground. The route viewing allows you to absorb as much information as possible, predict the scenarios for each part of the climb and make a plan to deal with them.

The next stage of your preparation for a bold lead is to be aware of all your options to escape any part of the route. Here is the crucial difference from safe routes. On safe routes, it's all about falling technique and familiarity. On bold trad, options to escape replace falling as the means of safe failure/retreat from the route. Again, gaining familiarity with these is about awareness of the possible techniques and familiarity with them, as well as planning how they might be used on the climb you are about to try. Here are some ways to escape a bold trad route:

- Stay where you are and have someone lower a top rope.
- Stay where you are and keep searching for protection until you find it.

- Stay where you are until you calm down and are ready to climb on.
- Downclimb to the ground.
- Downclimb to the last piece of gear.
- Downclimb to a position where it's safe to fall on to the last piece of gear.
- Downclimb to a rest where you can buy time to think of other options.
- Keep going, you are committed.

Obviously the last option is the one that trad climbers fear the most (but also search for, paradoxically). If you are not aware of all the other options, bold trad climbing feels like only the 'committed' option is available most of the time. In actual fact, it's possible to keep this option to being a very rare and momentary occurrence. There are almost always one or more of the other options available. Practicing all of them in your regular trad climbing is the key to being able to actually use them, both as weapons to underpin your leading confidence and acting them out in real situations. Some are used much more than others. For example, downclimbing back to rests or to the ground is used on nearly every hard trad onsight. Top rope rescue almost never needs to be used if all the other strategies are employed. However, it is still used every single time by the mind, which understands the option is there if all else fails. This really helps.

Knowledge and practice of escape skills from bold trad climbs will make so many more trad climbs possible. They are used to maximum effect when included in the route viewing and planning immediately before starting up a specific route. Break the route into sections, split by changes in rock features, rests or obvious gear placements. The available options are likely to change at these points on routes. Even on the hardest and boldest trad climbs, the sections with only a couple of escape options available, or the final one; pure commitment, should be very limited. An example:

I was planning a 'headpoint' style second ascent of 'If Six Was Nine', E9 6c, in the English Lake District. Its reputation as a potentially deadly route and as one of the most dangerous trad climbs in the world was burned into my mind from the stories I'd read about its first ascent by Dave Birkett, and the stats from the route. Very sustained F8a+ climbing up a smooth overhanging wall, culminating in an off-balance tenuous slap to a hard-to-see hold right at the end. The crux comes right where your forearms are tiring, where fear is likely to be sneaking into your mind and where the fall would have the worst possible consequences. How would it be possible to keep completely focused without a shade of panic right through the whole climb, your life depending on maintaining it through that last move? Because you wouldn't have to.

In fact, you only need that focus for about 0.5 of a second. That's why you don't need to have a death wish to venture onto this route, just the right skills and plan. The breakdown of the plan is this: after the initial easy wall to a ledge, the first 5 metres is very bouldery, without gear that would stop you landing square on the ledge. This part is treated as a highball boulder problem. If you fall here, the plan would be to push out as far as possible, almost clearing the ledge, so that you could land dynamically on your feet and continue over the side of the ledge until the gear came tight. If that doesn't sound too appealing to you, understand that it really doesn't have to. You are not intending to actually act it out. Having the plan removes the unknown and reduces the worst case scenario for this fall in your imagination to a broken ankle and not something much worse.

Above, there is a good peg, the only solid runner on the hard part of the climb. So the following five metres of desperate climbing are merely sport climbing. Falling is safe and retreat, if needed, would be simply to jump or fall off in safety. Then, a much poorer peg above would hold body weight (proved by testing from the abseil rope), but probably not a fall. However, the section passing this runner and up to the crux move is a little easier. Even though you are getting pumped through this section, reversing a few moves to lower off from the peg is the available escape. In fact, reversing would be possible right up until you are about to make the crux reach. The moment you go for this move, the options instantly disappear bar one: complete the move or probably die. Any panic present in your mind when arriving at this move would make the prospect unbearably scary and tighten up your movements enough to make the worst case scenario a lot more likely. However, there is no need to arrive at the move in panic, because none of the climbing up to here was committing and can be done in relaxed, confident focus. The final decision to commit to that move happens at the preceding move and is only taken if you feel you have enough strength left in reserve to complete it safely. That was the plan, that's what happened and I did the move without much fear. For the half-second I was reaching for the hold, my life depended on success with no other options. High stakes for the mind to deal with, but reducing that feeling of commitment to such a short duration made it possible to deal with while making good, positive, confident decisions.

There are plenty of moments in bold trad climbing where you can't get away with falling off. Yet there are few where you cannot retreat. The key to success in this game is to extend your last point of retreat further and further with the tactics described above, and never go past it.

Part 4
The other big four:

attitude
lifestyle
circumstances
tactics

There is a big problem for those that do climbing or sport in general at a 'recreational' level, i.e. within a wider context of other interests in their lives like careers, families, other sports or hobbies. They tend to see climbing inside the frame of the time they have devoted to it in their routine. So when imagining ways to improve their climbing standard, the thinking is limited purely to what happens inside the weekly climbing sessions. However, there are small and quite painless changes to the general routine, circumstances or lifestyle that are likely to really matter for these climbers because they've already milked a lot of improvement from the stuff that happens during the actual climbing.

Of course, there are even bigger rewards for those willing to make more significant changes to their routine to maximise improvements in their climbing, such as their choice of job, the stress it produces, their diet and sleep pattern and the total time devoted to the climbing. This level of commitment is not for everyone. But don't miss out on beneficial changes just for lack of imagination to actually consider them.

We also inherit a set of attitudes and tactics from our upbringing and the environment around us that can either help or hinder us in dealing with the climbing challenge. It's certainly not easy to alter these, but it can be done and indeed it might need to be done for other improvements to begin. A large proportion of climbers are not using ideal psychological approaches for learning about climbing, absorbing its frustrations and maintaining a mindset that sets you up to find the solutions to barriers in improvement. As well as the psychological approach to improvement, the acute psychological state during climbing is clearly extremely important too. It has been suggested by sports psychologists that 60-90% of variance in performance comes down to psychological factors. Of course this is debatable. Perhaps a more helpful way to underline the importance of psychology is to see it as a link in the chain, and that psychological factors are needed to add leverage to other kinds of performance components like physical prowess.

Finally, tactical errors in your performances in climbing are all too frequently enough to sabotage your chances of getting to the belay, no matter how well you climb or strong and fit you are. A good awareness not only of the tactical levers open to you, but also the power of them, prevents big goals ending up at the mercy of little things like not having enough skin on your fingertips.

I'm young, spoon-feed me!

Sixteen (or thereabouts) year-old climbers are sometimes barking up completely the wrong tree when worrying about what's holding their climbing back. They worry that they aren't getting strong quickly enough, not realising they are already strong enough to soar past their immediate goals. They worry about lack of access to facilities, not realising that they nearly always have more power to change the facilities than they realise. And they worry about how hard their mates are climbing compared to them, not realising that their peers in the next city or country are climbing 5 grades harder.

However, they aren't worrying about the main problem they have: how slowly they are turning into good athletes. So what is a good athlete? Young athletes look to those around them who are performing well right now - the talents who are doing well for their age and have 'so much potential'. Yet here is the mistake that's only obvious in hindsight. The raw talents in mid teens rarely are the best in ten years time. They are good raw talents, not good athletes. So who is? The good climbing athletes are the climbers who understand earliest that no one else can do the learning for them. That unless they start finding the answers to their own questions they get stuck, just when they need to be making fast progress. Young athletes in some other sports have it easier than us climbers. They have a lot of access to regular decent coaching - someone to ask and solve the problems, hurdles and decisions that crop up along the way.

Climbing is changing fast in this respect. More coaching is becoming available for young climbers, especially in the indoor climbing scene. This is great, the young can learn a lot from their coaches very quickly, and jump ahead in their progress. However, even some of the best coaches around don't have enough contact or the inclination to teach possibly the most critical skill for climbers to have a long, successful and injury-free life of climbing: how to coach themselves.

This problem runs in parallel, and is indeed caused by a similar issue in the wider world of education. A lot of what schools teach works in the wrong direction for athletes who must coach themselves. Sure, they value hard work, focus and learning knowledge and skills, which are all essential. But they also value fitting in. By definition, athletes who want to be successful cannot and should not fit in to their surroundings - they must stand out. They have to look at the standard of effort, or even just the type of activities that 'everyone else' does, and not be scared to do something different. Different can mean the opposite of what everyone else is doing, or more of the same things. It doesn't matter. It's more than just knowing that it's okay to do something different, it's also knowing when to do something different.

In the 'real' world of academic success and careers, those who get furthest, earliest are the ones who move past expecting their teachers, mentors and 'the system' to spoon feed the answers to problems. In climbing, coaches, books and peers who can deliver the correct decisions on what to do next in your climbing are few and far between. So the earlier this skill is developed, the fewer wrong turns you make and the less you have to pay for them with injuries and plateaux in improvement.

The lesson here is that young climbers should worry less about squeezing extra percentage points out of their rate of strength and fitness improvement and more about developing the critical thinking and knowledge of the science underlying climbing. The latter is what will play the greater part in their achievements down the line. Being a good climber today still means being a self-coach. And coaches are more than just athletes who don't perform anymore and teach instead. They use deep knowledge of the components of performance in their sport together with skill to apply them correctly for the novel situations and circumstances of athletes, in order to tread the best path through problems and make optimum progress.

Why mid-teens drop off the radar

Young, fit and psyched climbers are great at winning battles, but many of them haven't learned to win wars. Long and successful climbing careers are like wars. Few people get to the other end without giving up or slowing down because they can't get past the many small failures and get back up and keep going until the success finally arrives. So where do all those psyched youngsters you see at every climbing wall go to? Why do so few of them turn into the fully grown climbing super stars they could be?

What happens is this. Young climbers start under the encouragement of parents and friends, often at their local climbing wall. They fall in love with the sport and spend the next 2-10 years doing it nearly every day. They become the best among their peers, who praise them and recognise and respect their ability. They compete in local climbing competitions and win. Their parents are impressed. Relatives and teachers too are happy to see them do well. They practically live in the climbing wall or at their local crags. These places are their world of climbing. And for virtually all the time they've spent in it, they have been the best. What's more, everyone around them (who live in the same sub-world of the local climbing scene) constantly remind them they are the best.

Then, at about age 14-17, it's time to move outside this arena and go on a trip to a famous climbing area, or a national or even international competition. This is a defining moment. A very few will do well, first time. Nearly everyone else in this situation will get a huge, depressing shock. They were the best in their world of climbing, but now they've entered a bigger one, a different arena, they are almost the worst!

For a few, the shock is a big enough setback to take the wind completely out of their sails and decide that the pressure of trying to be really good at their sport is not for them. For the majority, the shock is unpleasant, but they respond well and keep going into the next stage of their climbing. That next stage is the real battleground. Comparing yourself in that new wider arena is much harder - no matter how hard you push, there is always someone working that little bit harder or more talented. For every route you trained hard for and nailed, there are three more you just can't seem to manage. Where every month, even every week of training used to bring steady improvement, now the gains come so slowly and intermittently you can hardly notice them. No matter how much work you put in, you can never regain the sort of improvements that came so easily when you started.

As this seemingly endless battle to make inches of progress plays out, almost everyone gets weary. One by one they reel in their expectations and ambitions or refocus their dreams on things outside of their sport. All this is normal, because not everyone likes the relentlessness of trying to get to a really high level in sport. The few who do will succeed in changing their outlook and expectations as they grow and progress to achieve all of their climbing dreams and ambitions.

118

So what is the attitude of the few who manage this? First: they manage to shed dependence on regular successes and praise from others. In fact, some personalities will even grow to avoid letting others know about their successes, lest it interferes with their motivation. Instead, they grow to enjoy the work and struggles. Instead of seeing their preparation and training as the annoying necessary evil to get the big reward at the end, they focus on the small daily successes. They learn to congratulate themselves for persistence, rather than its results. They relish new hurdles and find revelling for too long in the pleasure of achieving each climbing goal a poor match for the excitement of starting their next challenge.

Those who start climbing and find they are not as talented or strong right from the start should take heart at this phenomenon of sport progression. The longer they keep at it, the more the playing field tips in their favour. Struggling from day one teaches you early to enjoy the moment of small, daily successes, even if that's just that you kept showing up and gave it everything. This is perfect training for later and higher up the grade ladder, when the ability to enjoy the battle is everything and victories become ever more hard won. By the time you really need this skill, you'll have it perfected. It's right at that moment when the raw talents run into problems. The talents can overcome this as well, by learning to measure and value real effort and application in themselves. It's very easy to sit back and ride the wave of your own raw movement and strength talent while it runs. However, the rest will learn to apply themselves diligently to their weaknesses and catch up. Learn from them now, not when it's a bit late.

"I can't do that" he said, mistakenly

A lot of this book is about making you step back from the coal face you are chipping away at, and think whether there is a better area of performance in which to make more significant progress with your climbing. However, don't mistake this as an argument to down tools in one aspect of performance and replace it with another, just because results seem frustratingly slow to come. Judging the moment when the focus of your efforts is no longer going to get you any closer to your goal such as a particular route, or a level of strength takes the skill of a master to perfect. Only a few will ever manage to anticipate this moment. Most will only realise it once it's already happened, but the earlier we do, the less time is wasted.

119

People tend to stick way too long with one area where they are most comfortable working in. Examples might be crimping instead of attacking your weak openhanded grip, or getting better at clipping from below instead of clipping from an easier position higher up. On the rare occasions when they do try something new or uncomfortable they've been putting off, or work harder than they normally would, the opposite problem occurs. They give up too soon.

But not way too soon. When people are determined enough to try the new thing, like practicing falling, they do so because they are genuinely determined to achieve a breakthrough. So they go pretty far and don't give up easily. In fact, they usually give up when they are almost there.

Being almost there is the most vulnerable place to be on any improvement curve. Deep in the symptoms of the struggle, with the lightness of starting out and the rapid gains of early sessions faint in the memory, it's really hard to sense the proximity of success. Let's use fear of falling again as our example. The first sessions of throwing yourself off sport routes were utterly terrifying. After a few weeks, they are merely unpleasant. After a concerted effort to include falls in every session for several months, rather annoyingly it still feels unpleasant! The training takes time, it feels inconvenient and it's not much fun. Worse than that; now it feels like it's just stopped working. You are used to measuring noticeable improvements in weeks, but now its been months with virtually none.

It's easy to conclude that the fear is unbeatable - you are just not cut out to be a bold climber who can fall fearlessly. It's a completely natural thing to think at this moment and it seems to be confirmed by all the symptoms you are feeling with every session you work on it. There are no messages feeding back from your efforts which confirm that although it's hard going, you are getting closer. In fact, you are nearly there. You are almost at a point where fear of falling gets so low that you can naturally include falls in your regular climbing without really thinking about it. It's just automatic: a habit you don't really notice like your climbing movement style.

Once you reach that magic stage with fear of falling, you score a huge win. Unless you really blow it and avoid falls for some other reason for a long time, you'll never have to go through this pain again of fighting all the way from fear to confidence. However, giving up when you are almost there means going back almost to the start. Even worse, maybe you'll be stuck on that painful ladder indefinitely, switching between the pain of needing to solve this problem and making an effort, and the pain of giving in and and sliding back down the ladder for the umpteenth time. So it's really worth it.

So how do you get through the crisis of confidence when you are nearly there? The first thing is to know the difference between can't and won't. Seemingly endless practice or effort that yet hasn't delivered the result makes us think, "I can't take this anymore, I have to stop here". That's the language we are used to using, so we believe it and act it out. However, the conclusion is incorrect. What's actually happened is, "I am really struggling and I've reached a point where the pain of keeping going feels like it's outweighing the chances of getting a result". The latter is the truth of the matter, but it doesn't express our emotions nearly so well. This is damn frustrating!

The first stage to getting unstuck is to step back and not let our negative emotions translate into a self-fulfilling prophecy. No matter how painful or frustrating the effort is, you still have the choice to keep going. "I feel like I can't take this anymore, I'm really not sure I should keep going". This is subtly different, but it recognises you have a choice to make. You are not being forced into failure.

To make the right choice, more information is needed. Is it really pointless to carry on? The symptoms of the effort: fatigue, monotony and frustration are all easy to sense. Instead, what messages can you think of that measure what progress you have made? How much more improvement is needed to get there? How does this compare to how far you've come? Answering these questions usually gives a clearer sense of where you are and a better perspective to balance out the raw emotions. Remember that with many processes in training or doing climbing, the most painful moment is right before the breakthrough. So the worse it feels, the closer you must be. Are you ready to give up so close to payback?

So you've been practicing your falls for nearly a year, day in, day out, but still you go to a new crag or a hard onsight with some spaced bolts or out of sight of the belayer and the fear is back. Why haven't you beaten it yet? You are already fine with falling and rarely think about it when it's at your local wall, your usual crags and a handful of routes you thought were too scary to try before. So you are nearly there. You wouldn't even be on this route if you hadn't made all that progress.

Making the right decision about whether to stick or quit means measuring successes as well as listening to the symptoms of the struggle that shout the loudest.

Too old to improve?

Don't kid yourself about age. It's a handy excuse to give in and settle for an easy life, but be clear: unless you are among the tiny minority who are up there as world class performers or you have a catastrophic injury, decline in performance is a choice, even if you don't realise it. For athletes in sports that are strongly based in strength or fitness like running, a good career progression would be 10 years to get used to training, another 10 to reach potential, and then another 5 holding onto that high plateau clocking up successes before the very slow decline in form (but still capable of pulling wins out of the bag!).

Most really successful athletes might start that process at, say, age 5. If you started it at 15 or 18, it's not such a big problem. Starters this late would need a near optimum progression of ideal coaching, training and raw talent to have any chance of giving Usain Bolt a run for his money. But even he had a shaky history of progression that someone else could improve on.

Thankfully, climbing is not strongly based in pure strength and fitness. Performing well at climbing requires a big spread of technical and tactical skills as well as the strength, fitness and body composition elements. So the old 'uns have much more of a chance than in other sports.

So maybe a climbing progression could be 10 years to get used to training, another 10 to get to the strength/fitness plateau and another 10 to keep learning how to climb really well and be a savvy tactical master. Start at age 10, peak at 40 and hold on to that top form until 50. I'm being slightly flippant here, but it is perfectly possible and recent examples like McClure, Haston, Hirayama, Zanolla and many others I could list demonstrate it for you. Thanks to them for their inspiration!

The 40+ or even sometimes the 30+ worry they can't get better because in general, their peers are getting worse. It's a mistake.

Those who discovered climbing in middle age, or return to it after a couple of decades concentrating on family life are generally not trying to climb 9b. They just want to improve. The message here is that it's not the body holding you back. It will still respond if you stimulate it. Athletes in climbing don't go downhill because old age is limiting their responsiveness to training or they've reached their potential. It's because of completely different reasons, like these:

- They forget how to believe in their own ability to break barriers.
- They settle for an easy life.
- They assume that they can't get better, so don't really try to.
- They get injured and don't work hard to recover from it.
- Their priorities change and climbing no longer seems important.
- They let a job dictate climbing out of their lives.
- They lived for today in their teens and 20's and didn't set their lives up to keep having spare time in their 30's and beyond.

Besides these reasons there are many more. The primary hurdle when coaching older climbers is always the first one - to convince them that age is not the biggest barrier.

Except for injury. Injury is the one aspect that is hard to manage in a long career in sport. The effects of aging, together with inevitable accidents over time are to blame. Notice that key word though - manage. Injuries are hard to manage, but are rarely impossible to beat. There are plenty of stories available of old climbers beating horrific injuries to reach new grade highpoints late in life. Hardly anyone rehabilitates injuries. It's not in the culture. It gets too expensive and apparently risky (for club shareholders) to put old pro footballers through injury rehab, so they throw them on the scrap heap. They have no choice, they need picked for a team. Climbers have a choice though. They can be patient, keep going through long rehab and come out of the other side. It's about application and determination. Seek out good advice, put in the work, recover and get your hard climbing back.

Climbers returning to the sport after a break of many years have probably the hardest time here, because they are always comparing present performance to previous highpoints of fitness. When those highpoints don't reappear quickly after resuming climbing, they are too quick to conclude they are unattainable. They almost certainly aren't, but they will take time. What will be different now to your twenties is that your body will hurt and complain if you don't treat it well. Before you would barely notice. Now, you'll have to be twice as diligent in warming up, carefully adding intensity and resting well with good food, sleep and relaxation to deal with the increase in work for the body. No doubt you'll pick up injuries on the way. Figure out what's causing them and correct it sooner rather than later. Don't make needless worry about the urgency of age make you try to progress too fast. Enjoy steady progress. And remember to look at all angles - twenty years of absence from sport might have produced some extra weight that needs shifting. All your old partners are away or out of touch. You'll need to make some new ones. It's never been easier with the internet and climbing walls full of folk in the same boat. Make sure the mix includes some young climbers - feed off their energy and enthusiasm and combine it with your experience and diligence.

Don't let your hard climbing career slip because you feel you have no choice. Choosing to keep it going won't be the easy choice - it's the hardest choice and the most rewarding.

But it is a choice.

To find time, make your time work harder for you

A big message from parts 2 and 3 of this book is that if you're focused on the right goal for improvement (whichever skill you are weakest at) then improvement can happen pretty fast. So it's possible to make gains that nearly any climber would be happy with, despite not too much available time for climbing. The paradox is that those with the most time for climbing, who live very frugally to climb virtually full time are rarely the best climbers. There seems to be a relationship of human effort that the more time is available to achieve a given task, the more of that time is wasted. Perhaps wasted is too strong a word. It might be part of the pleasure to take it easy and improve in your own time. My point here is that those with a busy schedule of career, family and other interests are often highly skilled at achieving tasks very efficiently. You can apply this skill to climbing as in any other field.

If you can count your available climbing hours in the week on two hands or less and you don't have many years of climbing behind you, the biggest challenge is fitting in volume of moves completed which is a big component of the rate of technique learning. That said, hardly any climbers do proper drills or seek out some movement coaching to eliminate the trial and error in their technique and hence start to build the skills into their movements at an optimal rate. If you did, you could learn technique several-fold faster than many of your peers. Improving finger strength to weight ratio is rather different from movement technique. Although it also tends to increase slowly with training, it requires less time commitment. It is more about patience and diligence. For the really busy, a fingerboard will be an immensely valuable tool. Alternatively, if you can manage to set up a home bouldering wall, it's possible to reach the very highest grades in climbing despite a demanding full time job with long hours, such is its efficiency in training benefit vs time.

The hurdle that tends to catch busy climbers is not the limitations of their schedule, it's just imagination to arrange the training to fit in, and actually believing it's possible. It usually takes a chance first-hand meeting with someone else in the same boat who has made it happen, or a coach or friend to make the right suggestions to trigger the change in attitude. Once the climber can see a clear, practical route to fit more climbing or training into their schedule without significant sacrifice in other areas, the rest falls into place.

Examples:

- Another spare evening freed up would allow a trip to the local bouldering wall. Even better, a bouldering wall in the garage would allow 2 extra nights of intense 45 minute sessions that could be squeezed in without disrupting other engagements/routines.

- Combining 30 minutes fingerboard with cooking or watching TV each night adds up to a huge amount of very intense training over the course of a week. Rock rings in the gym at lunchtime would do the same job.

- Drills on the warm-up routes instead of thinking about work or what you had for tea, followed by a practice fall from the belay, followed by a review in your mind as you belay your partner.

- A 45 minute intense session of endurance circuits on a bouldering wall instead of a full day doing routes (which probably achieved less time in the right intensity range anyway).

Of course, there are limits to this and although there's no reason why climbers cannot see decent improvements on the most gruelling of schedules, being open to shifting circumstances around to fit the climbing is the next level. It might be painful in the short term or even just too risky at a given moment, but rearranging work-life to be more convenient for sessions climbing or even just for quick access to a climbing wall after work might be worth it in happiness in the long run. Of course it's a deeply personal choice.

A big problem here is the gap in understanding between those who have achieved athletic success and those who are attempting to. A very common attitude is to assume that "If I had as much time as the pros do for training and improvement, there would be no problem". The truth is, there are no real pros in climbing, in the sense that most people think. If you take a sample of elite climbers, the vast majority will work at least normal full time hours and fit all their training on top of this. A true professional athlete's schedule of work and training is an utterly relentless routine with every waking hour spent dedicated to the activity. The bottom line is, successful climbers succeed because they have worked harder.

Do you really want to be an athlete?

Although the majority of climbers could lever their present resources of time, facilities and skills better to aid improvement, ultimately the highest form of athletic achievement comes when there is leverage in the right direction plus sacrifice. This discussion is quite irrelevant to those who have much room to improve the quality of their training without having to do more of it. However, for those that are really serious about pushing themselves as far as they can in their sport, this does have to involve a willingness to do what others wouldn't.

People often read the biographies or interviews with their sporting heroes and try to use them as a mirror for their own struggle to improve. "I could do what they did!" This rarely works out. The best athletes often have something that 99% of everyone else doesn't. They love the 'grind'. They love the long, repetitive, drawn out and seemingly unrewarding years between the excitement of the novice and the success of being at the pinnacle of performance. They love getting beaten, set back, frustrated and being permanently knackered from hard effort. They might tell you they hate failures, but really they love them, or at least the threat of them, because it brings out the best in them.

For most people it isn't like this. Monotony and long uninterrupted grinding effort with only the uncertain chance of some good results a long time in the future turns most people off, soon after they try it. When most people tell you they hate failures, they really do. When they do fail, they try something else so they avoid the chance of having that feeling again. When athletes fail, they lean harder into the task.

The trouble when reading the words of athletes is they often don't even know they have this love of suffering. Or even if they do, they take it for granted and it goes without mentioning to them - because their peers (those they compete with) all share the same attributes.

So for others looking in, it might seem like it's simple to copy the same regimes, ideas, diets etc of heroes and thus reproduce what they have achieved. What normally happens is it quickly becomes too hard to sacrifice everything else. Your mates are going out for a beer. You already missed the last three nights out through training. Are you going to say no again? It's hard.

Most people settle for their circumstances and work within them, and that's fine because it's possible to get fairly close to your potential in sport while operating optimally inside pretty tight time and resource constraints. It's in the last few steps to get to the really top grades where the climbing needs to be prioritised over other things. Really successful athletes break the circumstances and force new ones, at a cost. The cost comes out of the other good things in life.

Being acutely aware of this dilemma does help though. It gives you the opportunity to look carefully at where your inherent character wants to be on the continuum between uncompromising athlete looking at everything through one dimension, or those that find the grind of improvement or the sacrifices of maximising potential too unpleasant. It's not possible to have it both ways, but you will find your place somewhere on the continuum. It's pretty hard to work against your inherent nature, but it's definitely possible to step quite far outside it's gravitational pull, if you have been able to see it for what it is. Remember you can also choose your moments to think and act like a stubborn, uncompromising, bull headed athlete. If you find yourself close to a big goal through diligent hard work and good quality preparation inside your normal schedule, you could arrange things so you can have some temporary 'holiday' from your other commitments like work to see the goal off with an uncompromising approach. But be careful, you might get addicted to this sort of behaviour!

Tactics often trump training

In general, climbers try to perform too much, even when they are training. However, as well as training the core elements of climbing like strength and movement technique, some time should be given to the tactics for performing on the real thing - the goal routes. For some climbers, the art of performing is limited to taking more rest days so the body is in good shape to give 100%, and trying as hard as possible in the moment of the climb. Yet, there is much more to performing than this. Tactics for the final performance often trump the effect of the training core elements. No matter how fit or strong you are or how well you move, if the conditions are bad, skin is bad, you haven't read the sequence, you mess up placing the gear or clipping the rope or you are too cold to produce a maximal physical effort, you'll still fail. Good tactics for performing are really just a combination of common sense and imagination for seeing all the possible ways to tip the scales in your favour on a climb. If you get into the habit of trying to imagine all the possible tactical advantages you could give yourself on every route you do, you'll develop a knack of thinking of them. Good tactical climbing is a way of thinking and approaching climbing as much as a set of specific pieces of knowledge. That said, there are some general tactics that apply in many climbing situations. Here is a list of tactics that are commonly absent or poor in climbers performances:

- Not timing the attempt for when conditions are best in the year/season/ day. Wait until it's as cool as possible without your hands going numb, for the best possible friction. The first time you really experience the effect of good friction is a revelation. You feel almost weightless. Getting this right is an art in certain climates. The trouble is you are aiming to achieve a contradictory balance of cool skin on your fingertips, but warm enough hands that they aren't numb and warm muscles that are ready to work hard on the climb. If the weather is warm and you have to wait a long time to cool down for a hard climb, you'll have to be careful your muscles don't cool down too much. Still, humid weather is hardest to deal with. Try to find somewhere with some wind. Even a slight breeze will cool your fingers down and allow you to keep a jacket on and keep muscles ready for action. If cold is the problem, try not to stop moving at all during the climbing day. If your core temperature falls quite far, it's hard to come back from and perform at your limit. If you have to belay for a long spell in the cold, go for a proper run in a big warm jacket to get your pulse rate high for several minutes before your turn to climb. Try to overdo it, and arrive back at your route overheating slightly. By the time you've geared up and got your rockshoes on you'll be coming to an ideal performing temperature.

- Not reading the sequence in onsight climbing. Climbers generally don't spend nearly enough time looking at their routes from the ground before attempting them. Of course not every route lends itself to it, but there are nearly always secrets it will give away if you take the time to walk around and stare at it from as many different vantage points as you can. Look for protection points, changes in angle, potential rests, obvious holds, sections that lack obvious holds (be ready to fight hardest here), chalked up holds, and thumb chalk prints that give away the hand sequence.

- Not reading the sequence in redpoint climbing. When working routes, climbers inexperienced in redpointing tend to settle for the first method for a given move that works. This is not necessarily the best way to do the move. Sure you can do it on it's own, but it might be hard enough to make you fail when you arrive at it pumped from linking the whole route. A more thorough and systematic approach really pays off and doesn't take much more time. When you find a method that works for a hard move, take another minute to try the other three or four most obvious options, different handholds or footholds. Even for experienced redpointers, you'll find an easier way half the time. If you progress to trying to link the route and fail on an unexpected move, or the same move all the time, rather than keeping on throwing yourself at the redpoint, take a step back and rework the move for a few minutes or more before trying the link again.

- Take the correct gear for the route. If it's a trad route, look carefully at the route and the description. Don't carry extra ballast that's not going to fit in the pitch just because you're used to carrying it. If it's a sport route, maybe your route viewing will inform you that you'll need most of the quickdraws on the left side of your harness. If you realise this mid route and run out of draws on one side, use time at a rest to move some more over to the other side.

- Time your eating and drinking so they don't interfere with your moment of battle on the route. Eating a lot, minutes before a hard climb might make you feel bloated or lethargic. It's very easy to let dehydration creep up during hot days climbing if you don't take regular breaks and keep water immediately to hand. It's also a common problem on cold days where you just don't feel like drinking.

More common sense tactics: Brush the holds clean of chalk and dirt. Make sure rockshoes are clean and dry. Take enough time to pack before leaving to climb. The simple act of packing helps to encourage more planning of the sequence of events and things to remember for the climbing day. Know what climbs your partner aims to do, discuss the best plan for the climbing day so you both make the most of conditions and energy. On very cold days for sport climbing it sometimes works to take it in turns to belay each other for a half day straight rather than alternate routes to stay warmed up between attempts. Watch other climbers on the route or videos of it if you aim to redpoint it and save energy when it comes to working out moves yourself. Know the situations that make you stressed or bring out the best in you. Maybe you like the pressure of the last day of a trip, or people shouting encouragement, or climbing with a particular partner for hard routes. Set up the correct conditions for you to be focused and happy for your moment on the route.

For some more advanced climbers, all of the above tactics will be obvious and second nature. For them, the tactical game will be more subtle. They look for small details that will tip the balance on the really hard routes. Maybe it's estimating how many attempts you have on a sharp hold before it cuts your fingertip. Maybe it's waiting for one really good attempt on a route in the best conditions just before dark instead of having three low probability attempts in the heat of the day. Maybe it's the right combination of gaining body heat from moving around and cool breeze to bring the fingers to the right temperature. Or maybe it's some change in your preparation routine at the crag that makes you more relaxed and ready to give it everything. Imagination, experimentation and curiosity for what your peers are doing will keep teaching you new tactics all the time.

What the warm-up does

Believe it or not, warming up it still not an entirely proven concept in sport, with a few pieces of research doubting it's efficacy. However, all the evidence from real life performance shows pretty overwhelmingly that it's essential to get the most out of your body and to work it hard without breaking it. It seems likely that part of the reason why the mechanism in which the warm-up works is difficult to tease out is that it's multifaceted. In general terms, it connects the various different channels and body systems that are called into action in the specific sport, and prepares them to work in unison.

The most talked about body system that is thought of when dealing with warm-up is the muscular system. The warm-up prepares the muscles for hard work by exciting them, pre-dilating the muscle circulation and raising it's temperature. There are also psychological effects that are an important part of the picture. The warm-up helps to clear the mind of other thoughts and distractions and fill it with the necessary elements and focus for a good climbing performance.

The pace and progression of the warm-up is critical to ensuring that it adequately prepares you for an optimal performance afterwards. In this case, optimal performance means either climbing at your limit, or simply being able to complete the planned training session. If the warm-up is too short or too light, the high intensity work following it will tend to tire you out much more rapidly than normal. The only exception to this can be for fit climbers having multiple days in a row during a phase of intense training or a climbing trip. In this case, the body seems to need less warming up to reach optimal readiness for performance than if there had been rest days. A shorter warm-up here might be a good tactical decision if it's possible as the glycogen fuel store, and hence the total volume of climbing time before exhaustion, might be running dangerously low.

Warm-up takes between five minutes and two hours depending on the individual, the conditions, recent history of activity and the type of climbing being done. The shortest warm-up will be extremely short duration strength activities like fingerboard. A bouldering warm-up will commonly take 20-60 minutes, and a warm-up for endurance climbs longer again and more gradual. Experience will inform you of how your body responds to different amounts of warming up for different types of session.

The content of the warm-up should be as specific as possible to the activity. So if it can be done by climbing, that's great. So the first activity of a climbing wall session should probably be just an easy route or moving around on big holds. Some advocate a lot of additional work such as general pulse raising aerobic work. This will certainly be useful for climbing in very cold conditions to pre-warm the body ready for exercise, but it shouldn't be necessary in warm conditions. Stretching does a similar job to simply using the muscles - it increases blood flow and warms the muscle. So, again, simply doing some easy climbing should be sufficient. However, stretching is certainly advisable for injuries which respond well to a more gentle start to the session and may have shortened and stiffened if scar tissue is being laid down in recovery. Try to make a smooth progression of boulder problems or routes, getting more difficult, until the final warm-up route really tests muscular recruitment in bouldering or gives a good pump in endurance climbing. However, the body will not like being pushed too far too soon. If you try a warm-up route that's too hard and carry on fighting to the top, it's often impossible to have a good session afterwards.

Tuning in and out

Sustaining the motivation to break barriers of effort and application during training and performing in climbing comes down to a combination of factors. In earlier parts of the book we've seen how understanding the effect of habits and preconceptions as well as seeing clear benefits on offer from changing them all contribute to your willingness to take your climbing to another level. There are also motivational barriers while you are actually doing climbing. The sheer effort of climbing and the sustained, occasionally monotonous nature of training for it is addictive for some, but highly demotivating for others. What can we do to make this easier on ourselves?

There are two psychological strategies commonly used by sportspeople in training or performance to help manage the tasks of working your body extremely hard, or completing sustained arduous training sessions. These are called 'association' and 'dissociation'. Both techniques, in different settings, have been convincingly proven to help increase performance or simply help you get to the end of an arduous training session. With association, the athlete focuses the mind on a particular aspect of the effort, such as heart rate, feedback from moving limbs and muscles, pain from muscle fatigue or even more subtle mood changes. The research shows that association helps athletes regulate effort and pace better in competition (performing) but not in training. The rationale for this is that motivation is really high during a performance that matters, so the pain of working hard doesn't feel so unpleasant. In climbing, the commonest form of association is to notice the changes in forearm pump or your breathing rate and depth, especially as you move your feet around. Other things will be changes in the dexterity and speed of your fingers as pump and fatigue sets in, the sensitivity of your fingertip skin on the rock and a general sense of the weight of your body against gravity. Tuning in to some or all of these subconsciously during fast movement or consciously at rests helps to monitor your level of fatigue and use this to make decisions about what to do next (climb faster, reassess danger, linger at a rest longer etc).

By contrast, dissociation is tuning out from certain physiological or psychological sensations to help perform better or for longer. Endurance athletes commonly use the technique in running to help them get through long, arduous bouts of effort or training sessions that would otherwise feel highly unpleasant to sustain. The research shows it's very useful in training for runners. The same doesn't hold true for performing since constant subtle adjustments are needed to achieve a personal best performance. The exception to this is with athletes at a lower level of fitness or ability, who are less used to the arduous nature of hard sporting performance and find that tuning out from 'the pain' is helpful.

Which to use in climbing? Most climbing situations have far too many moment to moment decisions to be made for dissociation to be effective. You have to be mentally 'there' and motivated to concentrate and try hard both to train and perform well in climbing. Individuals might be able to master a combination of both techniques at certain times. For instance, focusing (associating) on the sensation of moving limbs as you climb and breathing, while dissociating from the pain of sharp holds on worn out finger skin. Dissociation works better in a sport like running which is less dependent on ongoing movement technique decisions than climbing and more reliant on operating at a high level of exertion.

However, dissociation may have a place in endurance training in climbing at certain times. Endurance circuits where you know the moves, especially when done on a bouldering wall are an extremely effective way to make endurance gains. They are also very arduous and repetitive. Both the potential boredom factor, and the repeated painful nauseating forearm pump are the limiting step in the motivation of some to complete the training. Use of dissociation should help to manage this. Focusing on the rhythm of the moves, other thoughts or sensations you choose or even music in the background can help to achieve this. Meanwhile, detach your thoughts and focus as much as possible from the unpleasant sensations of the activity.

Dissociation is also used in management of fear in dangerous trad climbing. However, this is an extremely dangerous mental tool. Use it only after a focused, deliberate assessment of safety has been made. If you are choosing to commit yourself to a section of poorly protected moves, and are sure of your decision, then dissociation from fear may be the only way to complete the moves without interference from fear and panic (and therefore safely). However, as soon as the conditions change, association must be once again adopted to fully identify and assess danger.

Another dangerous use of dissociation is to ignore pain of developing injuries. This technique is commonly the cause of less serious injury developing into something much worse. In general, the mark of an athlete who stays healthy and injury free is constant use of association to be vigilant and monitor developing and existing injuries in any situation. Feedback from injuries and the decisions that flow from this is our only way to manage rehabilitation and training at the correct rate to maintain good health.

Managing the 'psyche' level

Psychological arousal, what's generally referred to in climbing as 'psyche', is a crucial tool for success on climbs near you limit. Generating high levels of mental arousal is not that hard - anyone can whip themselves up into a frenzy or a temper and attack a boulder problem like you want revenge. However, the result of this is generally failure due to the gross inefficiency of an uncontrolled explosion of effort. The real skill has three components: generating, timing and directing the psyche or effort.

High physical and mental arousal can be used either to help deliver those last few percentage points of muscle force, or to support some other mental technique such as shutting out fear, panic, or the pain of fatigue. The basic and still largely accepted model of the correct level of mental arousal, or anxiety is the 'inverted-U' model. Plotting anxiety level against performance, the graph forms an inverted U shape, in which a moderate level of anxiety is best for performance compared to either too little or too much. Today it's accepted that it's crucial to take account of individual personalities to find the optimal level of arousal. Some will work better than others under higher or lower levels of 'psyche'.

Climbing is not like many endurance sports, where a continuous level of arousal is needed, like in running or cycling. By contrast, on crux hand movements, we need high arousal to deliver near maximal muscular force, but at the very next moment it must be much lower to perform a delicate shift in balance, or a subtle foot placement. Often routes or longer boulder problems require maintenance of a fairly low physical arousal during most of the climb, with the purpose of saving energy for the crux. When you arrive at the crux, you must immediately reverse the strategy and raise the psyche level as high as possible without loss of accuracy in the movements. So the skill is in adaptability and timing of arousal level adjustments.

Climbers commonly fall on either side of the optimal level of psyche. Some climbers simply don't know how to work themselves up into a high level arousal to climb with aggression and focus. Others overuse their aggression in the mistaken belief that more is always better, especially in bouldering. They usually fail due to inefficiency or inaccuracy of their movements resulting from this explosion of aggression.

The climber will need a tool kit of psychological strategies and routines to help adjust the psyche for whole sessions, before attempts on routes and in the moment of single moves. An understanding that adaptability of psyche to match the immediate task is just as important as being able to generate psyche is also crucial. Internal decisions to adjust the arousal level in anticipation of the immediate climbing task are the core element of management of arousal. Supporting techniques include:

- Use of breathing techniques such as rapid breathing or sharp inhalation to 'tighten up' ready for a crux move.

- A pre-climb routine.

- Verbal encouragement from onlookers.

Successful rock climbing needs delivery of power and withholding of power at different moments. Train your ability to control your arousal level to match these needs.

Do you really want it to be easy?

The psychology of attempting difficult routes or boulder problems contains an awkward paradox. We look for difficulty, and want to be challenged, yet we get frustrated when success doesn't follow effort immediately. What if you could magic that extra edge when you got really frustrated with repeatedly getting close to a route, so you could finish it off? Would it make you a happy climber? Of course not. Because you'd immediately try something harder. The answer to the paradox is to focus on the performance, not the result. Being attached to definable successes such as routes or moves completed helps to structure our effort. But pinning everything on this has a detrimental effect on morale, because the goal isn't always possible at the moment we hoped for.

Instead, a balance of aiming to complete real, tangible goals like completing a route, with value based ones like concentrating hard, delivering maximum force or being very accurate with movements is the most satisfying. You'll see this in action when you unexpectedly complete a route despite knowing you climbed badly. It's a satisfaction tinged with emptiness. A valiant failure where you know you gave your all and climbed well is a vastly more fulfilling experience. Some would even say that it matches the level of satisfaction from succeeding on a climb.

Climbers also get frustrated by feeling like they were 'unlucky' to miss a hold or a foot slipped. But a focus on the quality of your performance sets you up to be 'lucky' more often. If you find yourself regularly bad tempered or bitterly frustrated with climbing, it probably has little to do with your skill level, and everything to do with your outlook on pushing yourself and the rewards from sport.

Be thick skinned at all times

The skin on our fingertips is the tiny area that our body comes into direct contact with the 'playing surface' in rock climbing. Think of how other sports treat this connection and how highly it's valued and optimised. Racing drivers obsess about the correct tyres for different conditions. In curling, the team prepare and adjust the frictional properties of the ice as the move is in progress. Tennis players are sensitive to miniscule changes in the distribution and level of tension in their racket surfaces. Even in rock climbing, the frictional properties of shoe rubber form one of the main marketing angles of shoe manufacturers. It makes a huge difference.

The massive jump in rock climbing standards when we started using chalk in the 1970's is obvious. However, the importance of managing the condition of our fingertip skin and how to go about it is still an emerging aspect of climbing knowledge, trickling down from the elite end of the sport.

Rule number one is to avoid splitting your tips (fingertip pads) at all costs. A split will need three or four days off to heal enough to handle small holds again, and even then will be prone to re-opening. Less days off sharply increase the risk of the cut reopening. Most of the time, splits are avoidable by observing your fingertip skin during a session. Repeated pulls on a small sharp hold will roll back layers of skin and warn you it will split soon. Climbers who take the holds with care and have clean technique tend to suffer from split tips a lot less.

As the skin wears from repeated pulls on a sharp hold, try to tear off any rolled back layers of skin as these tend to catch on the hold edge and tear the skin more easily. One tactic used often by boulderers is to work the moves of a sharp problem wearing finger tape wrapped over their fingertips to save skin for redpoint attempts once they have learned the moves. If you get a split, you'll probably have to stop climbing right away or make it much worse. Cover it as soon as possible with a breathable plaster to keep the area moist so it doesn't dry out and crack, lengthening the healing time considerably. You might need to use finger tape until you get home and then replace with a plaster. After a day of healing, remove the plaster, let the skin dry out for an hour or so and then sand down the edges of the split with a nail file to encourage new skin cells to knit across the gap faster. Sharp edges of skin at the split are extremely prone to cracking and making it worse before it gets better. Sanding down the skin so it's softer and more malleable really helps avoid this.

Poor conditions make you use up skin much faster than cool, dry conditions. Humid or warm air makes your fingertips permanently moist with sweat and susceptible to wear and tear much more easily on sharp edges. Try to climb in a breeze and wear light clothing to keep skin cool and hands dry. Keeping your hands chalked during short to medium length breaks between attempts helps maintain good skin for longer. Some boulderers even blow on their fingertips to prevent them becoming moist during rests. Between climbing sessions, try to avoid getting your hands wet for extended periods as this tends to soften the skin and prevent it from taking on a leathery consistency that works well for dealing with large volumes of climbing and rough rock.

Climbers have experimented with various methods to encourage skin growth during rest days. Good general recovery practice such as eating and sleeping well obviously helps. Of the various creams or ointments tried out by very active climbers, there have been reports from a few climbers of promising results from cow udder cream (I'm not making this up!). This is an ointment that is used by farmers on cows' udders that promotes skin growth and toughening to prevent the udders becoming chapped. Impressive lateral thinking by whichever climber thought of this first as an aid for toughening climbers' fingers. The major problem with it's use is that it tends to make the finger joint creases dry out and crack crack, causing long term and quite serious hacks that become engrained and refuse to heal. So those that have used it successfully apply it very carefully and sparingly to only the fingertip pads before bed, and sleep wearing cotton gloves. It might sound laughable, but some report that it's solved a major limitation in their climbing of having naturally very sweaty hands and sore skin during climbing as a result. The cream is rather hard to come by, but seems easier to find in the US. It has not been rigorously tested on climbers though, so further research is advised.

Occasionally, too much skin on the fingers can prove a problem under certain conditions. Climbing for many days back to back provides a strong stimulus for the skin to regenerate. Similarly, climbing on limestone tends to build up thick, leathery skin without wearing layers off as much as other rock types. If you are exposed to either stimuli for some time, then take a few days rest, then come back to a rock type that relies heavily on friction, you may find the skin is actually too thick and tough. It takes on a 'glassy' texture and it's hard to get reasonable friction on the rock. An immediate remedy is usually to dampen the skin and reapply chalk, rubbing it into the fingers to soften them and break up the smooth surface. The problem soon passes after a couple of hours climbing on rough rock.

Managing skin on climbing trips or during frequent training bouts is a real tactical challenge for climbers. Unfortunately, there are no easy answers and a lot of the time, it's necessary to play the game of preserving skin as much as possible and optimising the recovery as best you can. The key mistake on climbing trips is for climbers to be unrealistic about the effect of thin and sore skin on their climbing. It seems irritating if not embarrassing for the inexperienced to allow sore skin to get in the way of more climbing. However, the fact remains that it is a big factor in performance, and sometimes it pays to be patient and wait rather than try to ignore the pain even longer.

Does flexibility really matter?

Flexibility does have a place as one component among many that contribute to general climbing ability. However, the bottom line is that it's one of the smaller contributors. For those with an average level of flexibility it is rarely a weakness and even more rarely a stopper on a given move. The first obvious reason is that extreme joint angles that require good flexibility are only beneficial on a minority of moves. Even on these moves, it's often possible to use a slightly less flexibility dependent method with only a small loss of efficiency. Moreover, good flexibility is only consistently required around the hips. The two major challenges for hip flexibility in rock movement are high-steps and hip turn-out (adopting a 'frog' position on the rock). Of course there are some exceptions to this. Some male climbers with very muscular upper bodies lack flexibility to extend the shoulder in reaching and cross-through moves.

Quite a few climbers overrate the importance of flexibility and end up spending too much time training it through simple stretching or yoga which is more popular these days. With an abundance of available time to train this would be no problem because stretching uses little energy, aids recovery and yoga has other psychological benefits that will help the climber in addition to the increased range of movement. For most climbers though, available time to train definitely is limited, and flexibility training is quite likely to take away time from higher priority aspects such as more climbing or other aspects which improve finger strength to weight ratio etc.

The solution is first to assess the level of flexibility you have, especially at the hips and then to do some very focused stretching at times where you can fit it into existing training sessions. Another complicating factor to be aware of is the difference between active and passive flexibility. Passive flexibility is the range of motion you have by applying an external force to the limb (e.g. using your weight to stretch your hamstrings in a toe-touch). Active flexibility is the range of motion you have by moving that limb to the edge of the range without assistance. It's active flexibility that's important in most climbing situations. For example, to high step onto a foothold without having to move the rest of the body. Active flexibility is dependent on both flexibility and strength at extreme joint angles. It follows that training using moves such as high steps and pulling the legs into wide bridging positions is the best way to improve active flexibility, so long as sufficient passive flexibility is there.

If passive flexibility is poor, it will always place a ceiling on active flexibility. If your high step or hip turnout is poor, you should build stretches for these areas into your normal training sessions. There shouldn't be any need to add dedicated stretching sessions. Stretches performed while resting between routes, fingerboard sets etc are a very efficient way to clock up enough hours stretching. You do need to make a long term commitment to make noticeable gains in flexibility. So if you're serious, do it on every session.

The most effective method is to stretch the muscle out slowly over the course of 20-30 seconds, then relax for a further few seconds, then re-apply the stretch for a further 20-30 seconds. This progressive relaxation technique basically overrides the muscle's built in tendency to contract in response to being pushed beyond it's normal length, preventing damage. Aggressive stretching will trigger reflex contraction and renders the stretch useless. You should feel the tension in the muscle, but it should not be painful. Over time you'll develop a sensitivity for the correct stretch and awareness of when you've overdone it and the muscle fires in reflex response.

Any stretches that improve hamstring and inner thigh flexibility are the stretches to focus on, especially for male climbers. Sit on the floor with legs wide apart and lean forward to feel the stretch in the back and inside of the legs. Then sit against a wall with the legs pulled up and the soles of your feet touching each other. Use your arms to push your knees towards the floor to feel the inner thighs and hips stretch. Unless you have an additional flexibility problem, these two simple stretches might be all you need to do. Because the workload is low, you'll be able to clock up enough time on these two stretches that matter most during your normal climbing or training sessions.

Although an average level of flexibility in other body joints rarely becomes the limiting factor in climbing performance, one crucial consideration is injury. A rigorous stretching program for improving general flexibility might not be the best use of limited time to devote to climbing and training, but injury is a different case. Training muscles tends to gradually shorten them. Flexibility training done simply through normal climbing movements is usually enough to offset this. An exception tends to be those who use weights a lot. However, ligaments, tendons and muscles recovering from injury shorten much more markedly. Failing to stretch them rigorously not only prolongs recovery but sharply increases the risk of re-injury. This is because the injured structure is left shorter than the surrounding structures it works in parallel with. A shortened scar will bear the brunt of force from body movements instead of it being spread across various supporting structures. This will obviously risk tearing it. Injuries that suffer from repeated tearing of the scar form excess scar tissue that is weaker and less likely to recover fully. If you have an injury, stretch it as often as possible to encourage it to form a healthy scar that is the correct length.

Part 5
What's next coach?
Planning your improvement

Most of this book, in one way or another, is about how to stay close to the path of the basic laws of training, rather than breaking yourself against them with huge amounts of effort in an ineffective direction. The previous sections dealt with finding the right priorities to attack first and understanding why they might be more important for your climbing than for someone else. This section deals with how your improvement plays out over time, how to stay focused on the correct priorities as you make progress in them and manage the total amount of work so your body can stay healthy and not lose too much time to injury. The most basic idea in this area, and the one most often ignored is that improvement in any single performance component is not linear, it's curved.

Think curves, not lines

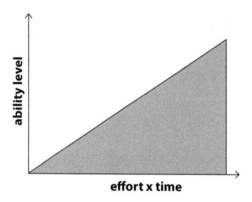

How improvement plays out in some people's imagination.

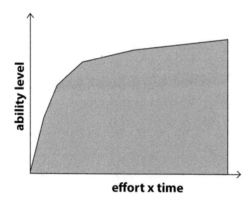

The real picture of improvement with effort and time.

You can see that on the right side of the plot, not much result is happening despite pouring ever larger resources in to that aspect of performance.

The second graph above is how our improvement rate tends to derive from the effort we put into improving over time. You can use it to depict a global measure like 'overall climbing ability'. However, it really becomes useful when we see that this relationship is occurring for each and every sub-set of abilities that make up general climbing ability. In other words, there is a separate graph for footwork, mental toughness, finger strength, move repertoire and all these very different things.

If we manage to put in enough time and effort to get onto the flat part of the ability curve in any one aspect of ability, we're going to have to pour vast amounts of hard work to get any further decent returns of improvement in that aspect. Instead, if we turn to another aspect where we are still on the steep part of the curve (a nice way of saying we're rubbish at it, don't you think?) we can go much further with less effort.

It's been said that climbing is difficult to train for because there are so many different ingredients that contribute to a good climbing performance. In fact this makes it easier with the approach described above, because only the real pro's ever need to be in that frustrating flat part of the curve in every aspect. I've never met a climber who fits this criteria. If climbing was largely about pure fitness, like running, training would be simpler, but with fewer avenues to turn to. The beauty of a multi-skilled sport like climbing is that you can come at your improvement from a different angle and still make good if not better gains than the areas you were concentrating in. So if you have great crimp strength, because you've trained it a lot by doing crimpy routes, you'll run into problems milking any more out of this area. It'll probably take a pulley injury to force you to realise it, but once you understand that fewer gains are coming from this area you can go and learn to really use your feet with clever heel and toe hooks, or get strong openhanded, or get light or a million other things you've neglected.

So jump off that plateau, if you can bear it

This all sounds very easy, but the problem is that the flat part of the curve - being a relative expert in one area (say, fingery boulder problems or runout slabs) is a psychologically comfortable place to be. Your performance from week to week is stable and good compared to your peers. You feel good about yourself and confident. This is the dangerous place to be if you're serious about getting better at climbing. Find a way to enjoy and relish finding new parts of the climbing game you are bad at and you will keep climbing the ability ladder at full speed.

The best climber is the one with the fewest performance areas still on the steep part of the curve. The game is to get as many skills or strengths onto the flat part where returns are becoming slow and petering out, and then move on. Your real energy should be in diving off that plateau onto another skill where you have a long way to go. This is another way of looking at periodisation which is the term for rotating the skills you work on in sport to keep the stimulus fresh and the body responsive.

The price of settling into the comfort of the areas you like working on is, at a minimum, a performance plateau. At worst, it is injury and loss of motivation. Maybe you understand that you have milked one skill as far as it can go but can't see what else to focus on. A good performance coach will undoubtably help you with this. If you don't fancy someone assessing your climbing, a good place to look for clues is simply to try some radically different styles of climbing. The fresh perspective usually gives you new insights into your own ability and flags up areas that are obviously weak you didn't notice in your normal routine of climbing. Travel to new places to climb, new crags, rock types, countries, even just a different climbing wall. Anything that's unfamiliar will help you see the picture of your own skills much more easily.

Regimes - how much can you handle?

When making decisions on how much training their bodies can handle without developing the symptoms of overtraining or injury, people often see only half the picture. They nearly always blame the training for the problems. Yet the chances are they could handle this volume of training no problem if they looked at the recovery too.

Ways to tweak the training to be kinder on the body:

- Vary the venue or the type of climbing. Twenty sessions at one climbing wall is likely to be harder on the body than ten at one and ten at another. And the latter will give better gains.

- Warm-up better. If it's cold at the crag make sure you raise your general body temperature high enough with some aerobic exercise in a warm jacket to buy yourself time to get moving on the rock before you chill again. If you stop for twenty minutes to chat at the wall, spend five warming up again before launching back in where you left off.

- Improve the conditions. Climbing in hot, humid environments wears your skin out faster and increases the frequency of nasty 'tweaks' caused by minor slips. If you have any control over the conditions you climb in, exercise it. At the very least, dress lightly to keep cool. Anyone with the luxury of a home bouldering wall will appreciate the huge difference a good electric fan makes for cooling and drying fingertip skin and preserving it through the session.

- Stop before you exhaust the glycogen store completely.

Ways to improve the recovery:

- Eat a healthy varied diet with particular attention to carbohydrate in the post training meal.

- Get a long, restful sleep, every night. Pay attention to the volume, routine and the conditions of sleep. A cool, dark and well ventilated room encourages good sleep. Relaxation before going to sleep and establishing a reliable routine of going to sleep at the same time each night is really important too. Adults should aim for 8 hours a night on average, but there is variability in this between people.

- Reduce the amount of general stress you place on yourself. General psychological stress as well as any other physical demands on your body are all combined with your training as a summative hormonal stress response. If stress is unavoidable then work hard to find ways to counteract it such as taking time for yourself to relax and enjoy yourself regularly.

- Minimise your alcohol intake. It really plays havoc with your recovery.

- Consider experimenting with other stress relieving or muscle recovery enhancing activities such as sports massage, stretching, yoga or other gentle sport. Running at 'conversational' gentle pace can actually lower the main stress hormone cortisol and can be very therapeutic for clearing the mind.

Above all, don't underestimate the cumulative, long term effects of poor recovery and management of training stress. It will put a lid on your improvement if you are ignorant of it. Treat your body nicely. Imagine that you are trying to persuade it to improve. If you take exquisite care of it (not just 'enough' care to get by), it will return the favour.

Over-resting or under-recovering?

As knowledge develops in sport, the new insights into training are not always perfectly interpreted and once applied in sport, conventions in practice linger long after the knowledge has moved on. Some decades ago the world of sport understood that the physical changes in the body that constituted the response to training occurred during the recovery period. Right as this was happening, athletes were suffering widely from serious injuries caused by overtraining that would seem crazy and reckless today. So clocking up rest days became fashionable and this was especially true among some groups of climbers in the early nineties. The pendulum of attitudes had perhaps swung a little too far back the other way. Climbers were training hard for one day at a time followed by three full rest days. This sort of schedule is actually not too bad for training bouldering strength and tends to give micro-trauma a chance to heal before it develops into an injury.

Nevertheless, it's going a little too far. It seems that smaller training doses interspersed with fairly short rest periods gives better results overall. The exact amount of rest needed for a given session depends entirely on the experience and makeup of the individual. Some climbers at a medium level will need two full days rest to recover from a session of strenuous climbing. In contrast, elite climbers might manage two sessions per day.

It's not really desirable to allow enough recovery to completely eliminate all symptoms of fatigue from the previous session to maximise gains, either for strength and particularly endurance training. If you are seeing your sessions as training, the best gain in the medium term will be from a sustained period of sessions with limited rest. This should be enough to depress your strength level noticeably, but it should be fairly stable. So, lets say your very best performance in a session is V12 if you are fully rested. During a training phase you might only be able to manage V10, but maintain this for 10 or 15 sessions with limited rest days. This sustained loading is the sort of strong stimulus that makes real progress in strength. It's not possible to do this forever though. Sooner or later (depending on your level) your performance will start to fall steadily from session to session and the risk of injury or overtraining rises sharply if you keep going. A good few rest days will refresh the body.

Cashing in

At this point, you have two choices. You can either start the whole process again and do another few weeks or more blocks of training to build up for a distant goal such as a trip at the end of the season. Or you can 'cash in' on this period of hard work and have a shorter period of less intense work with more rest days than normal. This rest should precipitate a performance 'peak' which you can use to go for a goal route you have been aiming for.

The above flexible structure is basic good practice in training periodisation. You have the choice of working yourself hard for longer periods for a big goal, or having more frequent, but less dramatic 'peaks' in a season or year. The worst position to be in is trying to 'peak' all the time, which unfortunately is a common mistake. Here, the climber rests for two or more days between each session in order to feel completely fresh for the next session. It works for a week or two, but beyond that endurance fitness and then eventually strength will start to deteriorate, not get better!

Taking all this into account, optimum recovery time between climbing/ training sessions is not a fixed quantity, it depends on the immediate goals.

A kid's regime

Climbers under 15 have some major differences from adult climbers that dictate a different approach to choosing the best content of the climbing routine. The first of these is they are still growing so have to be careful not to upset the course of growth spurts, or cause damage to growing bones and joints. Young climbers are often lured by the simplicity of gaining advantage by reducing body weight. It's a real mistake which could have severe costs in later life. They risk stunting growth through inadequate calorie intake to support growth at the optimum rate. They are also in a period where muscles and soft tissue growth is happening faster than at any other time in their lives due to the hormonal conditions of adolescence. Taking advantage of this and growing a strong, injury resistant body requires an adequate supply of calories and nutrients. Moreover, very low calorie intake can cause more serious interference with hormonal balance and opens up many more health risks.

The second issue for youngsters is the stress climbing places on joints, particularly the fingers while the growth plates at the end of bones are still active. Heavy, repetitive finger strength training in climbers under 16 such as campus boarding, fingerboarding and heavy reliance on crimping has been shown to result in bone deformities that cause painful inflammation swelling in the finger joints and can bring a premature end to the climber's career. Under 16's seem to be able to tolerate large volumes of difficult climbing and training so long as it is varied and not so stressful on the fingers. This makes good training sense anyway; movement skill learning is fastest in the younger years, so concentrating on gaining large volumes of moves completed rather than focusing on strength training (which tends to reduce the number of moves done per unit time) helps to achieve this. Young climbers can protect the future health of their fingers and other joints by weaning themselves off crimping all the time as quickly as possible, and sticking to the most efficient way to get strong for climbing (bouldering) until later.

Young climbers learn fast, so one of the most important factors for improving the rate of progression of children and young adolescent climbers appears to be the total volume of climbing (moves completed) and the variety of the stimulus. Different climbing walls, crags, climbing partners, mentors, coaches, videos or demonstrations and other forms of learning about what's important in climbing will all be absorbed more quickly than at any other time in life. Later in the teenage years it appears to be safer to begin to focus more on the strength and fitness development, when the body has developed the capacity to really respond, and respond fewer complications. But bones and joints are still developing until around age 20, and strenuous training before this will always be a trade off of benefits versus potential complications. There is no substitute here for individual monitoring and advice from professional sources, if you can access it. In an ideal world, this monitoring of a young athlete would come from a sports medic, a physiotherapist and a coach working together. Self-coached climbers will also have to educate themselves in the relevant areas of sports medicine.

A student's regime

The biggest single influence on successful progression in climbing through student life is the social norms and influences surrounding the climber. Of course, the social element is one of the very best parts of being a student. The trick, from the point of view of improving at climbing, is to take the best elements and moderate the worst. The best elements are an abundance and flexibility of time, opportunities to diversify the climbing, and a good network of keen partners. The worst elements are a recovery routine disrupted by poor diet, sleep and alcohol intake. Climbers often get their first finger injury during student days. Major contributing causes are climbing/training after poor recovery leading to accumulation of microscopic tissue damage or poor coordination due to the same reason leading to a sudden slip of the feet and loading of the fingers or elbow.

It's this period in life when climbers learn, the hard way, that their bodies are not bulletproof. They are actually very fragile if not treated well. In fact, climbing hard is an exceptionally arduous use of the body and must be matched by exceptional quality recovery to be sustainable without injury or plateau. Learning the hard way is everyone's prerogative, but you might feel differently when a finger goes 'PING!' and you need three months off your beloved sport for the sake of taking slightly better care of yourself.

The best answer is to have a routine, but a flexible one. Keep at least a rough mental note of your sleep pattern and try to avoid missing sleep. If you are staying out for the night after your climbing/training session, take time to have a good post training carbohydrate meal to prevent the immune system dip and get your recovery started. If the routine has been less than ideal for a few days, it's no problem, but you should reflect this in the climbing you take on. Do something less intense for a day like routes instead of bouldering.

The close knit scene of a student group or club can be fantastic for climbing, providing motivation and encouragement and immense enjoyment. However, make sure to let in some other influences to your climbing to diversify your outlook as well as your sources of technical and tactical habits.

A family/career hustler

One of the big practical problems that keeps climbers from their goals is how the whole picture of their participation in the sport fits into their life and leisure time. You'll hear lots of people talking about how, "climbing is not a sport, it's a way of life." In some senses this can be true, but as far as time spent doing it is concerned, work and family are the way of life, and climbing is the leisure escape. Earlier in the book we saw how some people end up with less available time to climb that they would like because they simply haven't decided to make it different, or don't even realise all the options open to them. Others have thought carefully about the allocation of their time and resources to the different areas of their life and have decided to fit climbing into a set routine and make the most of this. My point here is not that either direction is better, but simply that making the decision to do either is better than drifting on without really addressing it. Lots of climbers are regretful about not having more time to climb and blame lack of improvement on it, quite often unfairly. This situation is destructive for the motivation, and you end up not performing your best or enjoying either part of your life. Tackling your choices head on with regards to allocating time usually helps reach some new ideas about how to fit things together to get more done in the same time period. Moreover, accepting the time you have allocated to climbing in a positive way allows you to get on with thinking of ways to make the most of that time.

Here are a few workarounds for reaching your big goals in climbing inside a tight schedule, that will suit different personalities:

The temporary athlete

Sometimes, people feel they simply have to achieve a certain goal in climbing, or anything. Yet after a few abortive attempts, they realise they

151

don't have the 'bug' for the long grind of training and the athletic lifestyle. They desperately want to climb 8a or E4 or whatever, but not if it means a life of watching what you eat, missing social occasions, career opportunities, or even just having to try so hard every time you climb. Climbers I've coached often seem very embarrassed to admit this feeling.

I've seen some people successfully manage to skirt this deadlock of desires by being a temporary athlete. In other words, they get the athletic hard work 'out of the way' and then get back to 'normal'. This makes a lot of athletes happy when it works, and it definitely can.

Decide clearly what the goal is. The more defined it is, the better. Organise everything so you can literally drop out of life for however long it takes to achieve it, and go and do it. The hard work of training, dieting, no drinking etc won't feel hard "because it'll be over soon."

There are two ways to do this, either with a modest goal and going for it every few years, or every season. Some people will take some months off between jobs, or a whole year, or just sacrifice other leisure activities for a while in order to focus. Whatever suits. It also works for really massive goals, done once in a lifetime. Some folk will take a three year career break and go and do 8c, and then never climb anywhere near this level again, completely satisfied with doing it once. The great thing about this method is that in the process of the drop out period you might learn that you actually do have what it takes to juggle hard climbing and a busy life.

The focused weekend warrior

Beware the focused weekend warrior. At their best they can be among the fittest and most gritty athletes out there. They know exactly what they want, they know their resources and abilities really well and their time is precious, so they're gonna get that next hold because they can't come back tomorrow for another try.

The focused weekend warrior really wants to be the best sports person they can be, but they want a life too, a full life with a family and a good job. They can't give up either, but they've got a lot of energy and cleverness to throw at trying to have both. So long as you accept that it ultimately has a ceiling, this is a successful formula for many people. The only real downside is there's not much room for spontaneity in a schedule like this.

The advantages are that it does tend to focus the mind, not only in better thought out goal setting that sets you up for a motivation feeding series of cumulative small successes, but also in the moment of climbing, because the time is always now.

It's a demanding art form which only works when tightly managed by the organised. Keep things simple, don't pick goal routes that aren't in regular condition or a pain to get to. Get good reliable partners that think along the same lines and function as a good team together. Help each other. Get a good routine of training that everyone, especially your family understands and is happy with. It all comes down to being an efficient manager. The rest falls into place really.

The local

If you are the type of person who can do it, one strategy that works to clock up the climbing hours and ability without quitting your job is to move right next door to a climbing mecca. It has to be really right next door to work. More than 15 minutes is probably going to backfire and become a motivational black hole rather than cornucopia.

The specialist

Another strategy is to become either a temporary or permanent specialist in a single climbing discipline, so it simplifies everything and you can go much further up the ability ladder than if you did a bit of everything like most people do. I know many people who have done this with great effect in Scottish winter climbing. A smart tactical move here - choosing a discipline that takes the least number of hours of training to get to a decent level and most of the high value training happens in the mind.

It doesn't matter what strategy you go for. Choose whichever will make you happy. There are countless more ways. It's down to your imagination to juggle the pieces into place. It's clear there's more than one way to skin a cat when it comes to approaching long term climbing goals. Get more ideas from your colleagues who have the same job as you - how to they do it in their sports? What about your climbing partners? What elements of their strategy could you borrow?

The wannabe pro

For a proportion of ambitious climbers, a holy grail at the end of their climbing horizon is the image of becoming a 'professional climber', supporting a carefree life purely focused on achieving climbing goals. Along with this comes an idea that the climbers who are at the top of the sport right now have an advantage of unlimited time and resources to apply to their climbing success. Both these ideas are mistaken, and set you up for the wrong way to approach long term improvement and how to gain inspiration from climbing heroes.

Firstly, it's too easy to notice only the talents of famous climbers. The sacrifices, hard work and the length of time it took to get there is hidden. Broadly speaking, those climbers who have gone furthest have done so because they have been willing to work harder than anyone else. Any talent they have is nothing more than a catalyst - it was only the launching platform.

The second myth is that sponsorship is the ticket to an easy life and a permanent climbing holiday. It's true that some climbers can get close to this for a short time, sustaining it for a few years at most. However, it actually tends to shorten the climbing career, because putting off arranging your life for continued leisure time as other priorities emerge later on means you have to catch up, and there is less time to climb. The reality is that sponsorship is indeed a holy grail. The figures involved tend to be virtually non existent or nothing more than a little free equipment. Those few who move beyond this level of sponsorship receive it in return for adding more value - for working hard. This means speaking tours, writing, making film, shooting photography, going to events and meetings and staying in touch with companies. It's value for climbers comes purely from it's flexibility, definitely not from financial reward or less time commitment.

The truth is that all but a very few climbers would crack under the work commitment of professional athletes. This happens all the time to those who pursue it and discover the reality of it for themselves.

Obviously, the prospect of turning professional in climbing is only a discussion that applies to a few climbers. So why mention it? Their example is helpful to fully understand the reality of success in sport. Yes, talent is important. Yes, making the right choices is a critical ingredient. However, improvement at all levels is very closely correlated to hard work. It's important to see that there is nothing else. There are no favourable conditions like good sponsorship or talent that are even nearly big enough to replace hard work across years. The famous athletes are there because they said, "Another try!" instead of, "Time to go home, I'm tired!" and they did this week in week out for a couple of decades. That is a message for more than just wannabe pros.

The confused and disillusioned

Being on the flip side of improving at climbing - slipping back down the ladder of improvement - is a tough place to be. Even more so if it's not the first time you've been up and then down again. Some reasons why this happens:

- You had an injury that kept recurring.

- You took several years out of climbing to start a family or focus on a career.

- You lost a regular partner or handy access to a climbing facility.

- A long performance plateau destroyed your motivation to keep training/ trying.

When any of these happen and you lose ability you once had, it forces you to address an awkward question directly that you might never have really faced in your sporting experience.

"Why do I need to climb hard to enjoy climbing?"

Not many people can resolve a clear answer to it. Yet the sensation that the pain of lost ability is real, is highly unpleasant and possibly even more demotivating. It's only unpleasant because you might not have really thought about it before and realised what a big part good performance plays in your enjoyment of climbing.

When faced with this, some climbers become disillusioned; "I don't want to be dependent on my ability level in climbing to enjoy it!" Nonetheless, the feeling persists. The reluctance to accept it perhaps comes from seeing a dependence on ability level as being egotistical. It can be egotistical, but it doesn't need to be. The sense that your standing in terms of ability relative to other climbers justifies you as a worthwhile person is quite a shortsighted and ego centred idea. There are climbers who do feel this, or at least act it out without realising it. Ultimately, it's their loss not to see the wider picture of satisfying elements in climbing improvement. Linking public comparisons of performance to self-worth is only superficially and transiently satisfying because it's result based, not value based.

Improvement is deeply satisfying because it requires the exercise of good values: honesty, diligence, dedication, application, resourcefulness etc. Yes, it's hard to re-climb the improvement ladder, just to reach a summit you've previously stood on. However it's really just the concept of it that's hard to stomach. The action of it, in bringing out and exercising these values, will still be satisfying. Some reasons to get back on the ladder after a break:

- You'll feel good for making progress 'against the odds'.

- You'll end up being more focused on the truly satisfying elements of improvement (the values of it) rather than the results it brings. So it might make you happier than the first time round.

- Fewer of your peers will be so centred around the results of improvement as when everyone was younger. This is always a more open and enjoyable environment to do sport in.

- You'll be better able to 'live in the moment' of your time climbing, and spend less time dissatisfied and impatient with progress towards big goals.

- You'll develop more awareness of wider enjoyable aspects beyond results in climbing such as good company, the places you go to climb, etc.

Lower expectations will help you focus better on effort goals for the short term (today) and medium term. You might end up getting faster improvement than before because of this.

It's more common than you might think for climbers who succeed in returning to climbing and reassessing what they want out of it to surpass their previous level of performance. In fact, they are often happier doing it than those that have never been forced to examine the values they follow in climbing.

Same old routine, same old results

A common error in choosing the climbs to do to get better at climbing is to climb only routes at your current level. This is not the way training works. If 6a is your level and you climb only 6as in training, you are training to climb 6a. The trick is to start climbing on some 6bs. You are right to think this will cause some falls, some struggling and even some pain. That's the point. You have to force your body to respond. Naturally, you'll have to do a lot of 6bs before you get used to this level, and some easier routes so the body remembers the skills you have already learned.

This autumn, when you go back to the climbing wall for the winter season, instead of repeating what you did last year, get onto the harder routes. Struggle. Do one more session a week, add more bouldering, or fingerboard on the rest days. Do anything to avoid doing the same as last year.

Cracking bad habits is tough

Almost all of the changes to climbing routines I've recommended in this book necessitate breaking old habits and forming new ones. It's one thing knowing what you have to do and wanting to do it, but the final hurdle is to actually break free from old, engrained and comfortable habits. This is a lot easier said than done, so go easy on yourself if you take some attempts to manage it. Some thoughts that will encourage the will to see the process through:

Your current habits, techniques and routines feel comfortable right now, and the prospect of changing them seems uncomfortable. How will you last out under these psychologically unpleasant conditions? The main thing to remember is that new habits can and will feel just as comfortable once they are established. It's hard to see past the painful sounding elements of the new habit (regular falls, steeper routes, new angles or route types etc). Remember that the new habit has it's own set of enjoyable, comfortable elements that will provide their own gravity and hold you with less and less effort as time goes on. The painful bit is just the moment of change.

Allow for temporary failures. Hardly anyone makes an instant and flawless change to a new habit without any relapses along the way. When it does happen it's usually under conditions of great psychological pressure or fear. A common failure point in changing to new habits is when you have a relapse into the old habit and give in to a feeling that you just can't do it at all. Let some relapses go past you, but don't let it sabotage the whole effort.

Decide positively which strategy suits you. Some people prefer to jump in with a rapid and instant change of habits, going 'cold turkey' on the old methods to get past the painful transition process as quickly as possible. Other personalities will be overwhelmed and need to introduce the new ways gradually. It could be steep routes, leading, not overusing your clip stick, not saying "take" or grabbing another hold colour at the wall, or climbing in front of others. Choose the strategy that is most likely to work for you and go for it. Adopting the drip-drip strategy is often the hardest overall compared to jumping in at the deep end. It needs resolve to last longer and to go through more decision points of self-discipline. However, for the most stubbornly engrained habits it's sometimes the only way to get through.

Add external motivators to your momentum. Telling friends and family about an initiative you are taking with any aspect of your climbing makes it more real. It helps to add an extra force to get through moments when the path into your new habit is not going smoothly.

Keep the benefits in mind. Regularly reminding and restating the benefits of the change you are making plays a massive part in getting through a change of habits. This is especially true towards the later stages when the freshness of starting out or the pain of a low point in your climbing feels a bit more distant and it's easier to drift out of strong motivation.

If you try all of this and still can't crack the change, don't blame inability to achieve it. The reason for failure will lie in which tactics were used and how well they were applied. Make a plan for what you'd do next time and try again.

Rules of the training day

Earlier in the book we saw the 'structure of loading principle' which is that activities requiring the highest force output should come before lower force (endurance) activities. Following this principle allows us to manage the greatest amount of volume of activity and hence achieve the greatest training effect.

In applying it, it's important to be flexible and keep listening to the body for clues to what will be the best activity at any given moment. So, you may have decided that you are going to arrive at the climbing wall and do two hours of bouldering followed by one of endurance circuits - but what happens when you arrive and feel tired and sore from the previous session? Perhaps after a thorough warm-up you'll come through this and feel fine to boulder hard. However, if you still feel weak and muscles and tendons feel vulnerable to injury, it might be better to proceed straight to the endurance training, maybe even doing more of that than you intended, instead of the bouldering. This flexibility, led by body feedback, is critical for maximising the volume of training your body can deal with and avoiding injury. It might seem like you'll be getting less done on the day you have to take this choice, but the result will be much more done in the season. Less time will be lost to injury or just having to take more rest days because you've completely exhausted yourself. In listening to the body, take account of why you might be more tired than expected due to other stresses such as work or poor recovery from the last sessions. A single episode of poor recovery such as failing to replenish the glycogen store with a carbohydrate meal, a bad night's sleep or a big night out could linger on in poor training sessions for a week or more if you don't catch up on recovery.

So what are the messages from the body? An overall sense of tiredness is one. However, this is not enough on it's own because it can be very transient and the cause could be many disparate things such as just having eaten. A combination of messages should be used. Other ones are the soreness from muscles or rehabilitating injuries. Injuries are very useful measures of your recovery state because you tend to be acutely tuned into them through concern that it might get worse. The length of time to warm up and your level of strength on standard warm-up climbs is useful information. It's also important to notice how your level of strength and soreness is changing across a series of sessions. This is one of the main markers to decide if the intensity of your training is correct.

If you feel fresh and fully recovered with no muscle soreness and you are performing at your best, the general training load (intensity x volume) could be too low to make gains. This is fine if you are trying to peak right now to climb a hard route, but to make gains the body should be worked harder. If you feel the previous session in your muscles through a gentle stiffness or soreness - a feeling of them having been used well - this is good. You should notice this at its worst probably the morning after the training session and improving noticeably through the following day. It's fine to still feel some of this discomfort when you start the next session. It should dissipate at least a little after you warm-up again. The general feeling you are looking for in recovery is of significant soreness but the body 'bouncing back' rapidly. Although you will have some mild discomfort in the muscles almost constantly, your performance level during sessions would be relatively consistent, perhaps dropping only very slightly during the course of a one or two week stretch of heavy training for your level. If your grade or strength level is dropping steadily from session to session and soreness and tiredness are rising, then either the training load is too high or the recovery is too poor. Clearly, it's better for the training if you can improve the recovery quality by eating, sleeping and relaxing better and hold onto the high training load. However, in the short term at least, you might have to drop the training load a little before it forces it on you through exhaustion or injury.

This process of tinkering with training load, striving to optimise recovery and listening acutely to all the channels of body feedback is the constant activity of the training climber.

Rules of the training season

Making optimum progress across years in climbing requires prioritising the volume of stimulus in each component and paying attention to how each one responds to the loading. Finger strength responds very slowly with gains and is safest when done little and often. It follows that there should be some finger strength building activity most of the year. Some bouldering (or hard redpointing) for nearly the whole year is ideal. If your climbing circumstances don't lend themselves to this, then do as much bouldering as you can and just do some basic strength work on a fingerboard during the rest of the year when bouldering is not convenient. This dependence on a nearly constant diet of finger strength training is also true even for those specialising in sport routes. This is because being stronger (other things being equal) will translate to better endurance of a given difficulty of moves on routes; each single move will be a lower level of relative intensity. Sport or trad climbers can increase their diet of strength training without bouldering if they wish, by including hard redpoints into their activity. Some supplementary bouldering or basic strength work will really help however. Finger strength gains cannot be shortcut. It really pays to keep continuous activity going over seasons and years, slowly climbing the ladder of strength, step by step. The penalty for trying to shortcut the process with more intense training is severe - finger pulley and tendon injuries and inflamed finger joints. Quick fixes with finger strength backfire.

Endurance responds much more rapidly. Progress is measured in weeks, not years. However, these gains do start to level off more quickly. So the best strategy is to spend part of the year, maybe even the majority (depending on your goals) just maintaining endurance and focusing more on your foundation of finger strength, through bouldering or hard redpoints. When it comes to a month or two before you have big endurance route goals, you can drop the level of strength work and really fill your time with endurance volume to prepare for the goal. For those with very little time to climb, this period will be even shorter and building strength will offer better payback because the little and often schedule tends to fit better into very busy lives.

However, total volume of moves climbed is critical for technique too, so even the strength gains should be done largely on real climbing - bouldering first, but also hard redpoints of routes. If tactics and fear of falling are an issue for you, that will tend to make activities involving routes a better choice more often.

You can see that building a yearly schedule doesn't only come down to the type of climbs you are preparing for, it's also heavily dependent on the way technique, finger strength and endurance tend to respond to training and also the resources of time and facilities you have to work on them. All of these must be considered to make the best possible recipe for the yearly climbing diet that leads to solid improvement.

Annual rest and recuperation time

Incorporating annual rest periods into your climbing year to stay injury free and healthy is a popular idea among climbers. Is it a good thing to do?

The short answer is yes. Of course it's not possible to handle uninterrupted hard work of the same type indefinitely, and if you don't give that particular energy system/muscle group a rest every so often, it will force it on you through injury or stagnation sooner or later.

The mistake is to feel you need to rest the entire body or do something completely different to achieve the rest and recuperative period needed. Normally, doing some sport climbing if you've bouldered for months or some ice climbing if you've been clipping bolts all season is change enough for the body. There are very few people out there working themselves hard enough in every area to need to rest entirely, or to need something outside of climbing to keep them active during this recuperative period. For almost all of us, regular work and life 'stuff' gets in the way enough during the year to give us more than enough periodic rests. If you feel worn down at the end of a season, it's more likely due to the monotony of your sporting regime or wearing yourself out with insufficient rest or too much stress than the sheer volume of climbing you do. So, instead of hitting the couch, or pounding the pavements for a few weeks, try just mixing up the climbing a bit first.

Some suggestions:

- Go to a different climbing wall than normal for a few weeks. Or even just climb on a board/wall you normally avoid.
- Climb some slabs.
- Climb some trad.
- Climb some deep water solos.
- Do some ice climbing.
- Go on a trip into the mountains.
- Leave the guidebook (or maybe even the equipment) at home and go climbing by instinct for a while, without the need for hard routes. Just discovery and enjoy the place you're in.
- Hook up with a new climbing partner with a very different style to you.
- Completely re-shuffle the days in the week/session lengths/ venues and

activities you do in the week. Do the opposite.

If you still don't feel refreshed all of that, a good idea would be to do something that climbing is always getting in the way of - like lying on a beach for two weeks with your other half, or refurbishing your bathroom.

Summing up

If you've read all of this book in a oner, well done - books that get you to question your status quo non-stop are hard going. I'm guessing you'll have really noticed the huge range of subjects we've trawled through. From the correct number of seconds to hang on a fingerboard, to patterns of body movements and accelerations of limbs, to the attitudes and social habits of your mates. The ideal path to tread to get from beginner to mastery in climbing takes us through more fields of understanding, effort, learning and application than we probably bargained for. In each one, I've included just the raw details - the headlines. I'm hoping that I can answer your more involved and specific questions in several more books, films, blog posts and chats that have space to dig deeper in each area. My purpose with this book was to give you perspective. It was actually to draw climbers back from the details and see once again the whole picture of improvement in climbing.

I hope I have addressed the single biggest limitation holding back nearly all climbers in one way or another. They are lost in the details of a tiny subset of all the things that could improve their climbing ability. Worse, that subset might well be already milked dry and definitely the wrong battlefield to fight and win big improvements. Knowing more fine details within one area of climbing performance is unlikely to be the problem you need to deal with. For most, it never will be. This was the strongest lesson from my own experience as a climber trying to push myself and later studying the development of athletes generally through sport science.

If this book leaves you with more questions, great! Ask me them on my blog and I'll answer with more posts, books etc. If you ask any questions after reading this book, address at least this one to yourself: "Am I getting too deep into one area and distracting myself from another that might yield results that scale a lot quicker?" If the answer could be a yes, are you digging yourself into a cul-de-sac out of fear of the short term pain of attacking an area that scares you for whatever reason?

Climbing a move you know would have been impossible for you before is a magical feeling. So powerful, that you are willing to pour vast amounts of your time into learning and doing climbing, just for another taste of it. You had it a lot, but unpredictably and sporadically, when you first learned to climb. In later months and years in climbing, the gaps between these amazing moments get longer. But they become more predictable and dependable following a courageous head-on attack of your weakest areas. The only inertia working in opposition to this desire for breakthrough moments in climbing is fear. Fear of loss (of short term gratifications like being the expert in one small area), fear of effort and fear of failure. Getting past these isn't easy. The desire simply has to outweigh the short term pain. Knowing that pain will be short term really helps.

Once that happens, the real improvement can start.

Acknowledgements

Thanks to: Barbara MacLeod for generous editing time, advice and encouragement; Claire MacLeod for living with yet another obsession and her hard work to edit and produce the book; Alicia Hudelson for enthusiastic feedback on the text; readers of my blog who asked for this book to be written and provided excellent feedback and comments over the years and my coaching clients who have provided so many insights into the challenges and inventive solutions to climbing problems.

Dave MacLeod

Dave MacLeod is a climber based in the west highlands of Scotland. He is well known for his personal climbing achievements. He has climbed trad routes that have broken a new level of world class difficulty with Rhapsody E11 and Echo Wall E11. He has also climbed V13 in bouldering, 9a in sport climbing and XI in Scottish mixed climbing. His blog is one of the most popular climbers' blogs in the world and he has written extensively on training and improvement in climbing on his site and various other publications. His other main working activities are running a shop via his website, coaching climbers, and giving lectures. Dave and his wife Claire run Rare Breed Productions, making films, books and other creative things. Dave has a BSc in Physiology & sports science and an MSc in Medicine & science in sport & exercise.

www.davemacleod.com

Coming soon from Dave MacLeod

Climbing Injuries: Why you got injured again and what to do about it

Weight optimisation for climbers